David M. Schleser

Piranhas

Everything About Purchase,
Nutrition, Behavior,
and Breeding

BARRON'S

3

INTRODUCTION

Worldwide, the word piranha *elicits greater name recognition than almost any other group of fish. It might therefore come as a surprise that most of the commonly held beliefs concerning these species are either incomplete, oversimplified, or grossly inaccurate.*

Preface to Second Edition

Since the publication of the first edition of this book there have been many changes within the piranha-keeping hobby as well as piranha taxonomy. Most significant to hobbyists is the increasingly large number of species that are being regularly imported. Several new species have been recently described, and a few "species" have been divided into a complex of two or more closely related species (see *Serrasalmus spilopleura*, page 73). Although the true identities and ranges of some have been clarified, there is still significant disagreement on the identification and proper generic placement of others (see Genus *Pristobrycon*, page 84).

Much of this confusion can be attributed to the similar appearance of many species, profound changes in coloration and body shape (ontogenic changes) that many piranhas undergo as they mature, and the profound effects environmental factors and reproductive state can have on their coloration. Also lacking for most species is a broad series of preserved specimens from their entire known range that can be used for detailed comparisons.

In the hobby these identification problems are compounded by exporters and retailers frequently misidentifying piranhas in their tanks or tacking on made-up names of no scientific standing that they think might increase the fish's salability (i.e., diamond rhombeus, piranha muda, scarlet spilopleura, and so on).

Two species of piranhas can be seen in this catch: The larger red-bellied piranha, **Pygocentrus nattereri,** *and the more silvery and laterally compressed Sanchez's piranha,* **Serrasalmus sanchezi.** *Amazon River near mouth of Orosa River, Peru.*

The profound changes in appearance that many piranha species undergo as they mature are well illustrated by these photos of a juvenile (left) and adult (right) black piranhas, **Serrasalmus rhombeus.**

Within recent years, both field and laboratory research involving the biology of piranhas has greatly expanded our limited knowledge about these fishes. Studies using the science of molecular biology (DNA) have confirmed several long-held beliefs, such as the monophyletic (descended from a common ancestor) origin of

The word *piranha*, of Tupi-Guarani Indian derivation, has long been used throughout a large portion of these fish's range. In the Tupi language *pira* means "fish," whereas *ranha* (or *sanha*) refers to teeth. The correct pronunciation of the word *piranha* is pee-ron-yah, with the accent on the second syllable, and not the commonly heard *pir-ann-uh*.

piranhas, but have also raised unexpected questions. Even the exact number of species has yet to be determined. We are slowly beginning to understand their biology, behavior, and effect upon the other species that share their environment. One thing that has not changed is our fascination with piranhas and their popularity as aquarium fish. This has only increased as many lesser-known species have become more available. It is probable that within this small book's pages are pictures of more species of piranhas, many with collection data, than in any other scientific or hobbyist publication, past or present.

Origin of the Name Piranha

It has been written that the word *piranha* means "scissors" and that it was applied to these fish because of the resemblance of this cutting tool to their sharp teeth. The truth is exactly the opposite: It has long been the custom for Amazonian natives to use dried piranha jaws to make a tool that is intermediate between scissors and a knife. When these Indians were first shown a pair of scissors it is no wonder that they called them piranhas—a term still used in parts of South America. Piranhas

This beautiful yellow piranha caught in the Amazon River near Iquitos, Peru, is probably an undescribed species within the **S. rhombeus** *complex.*

were known by that name long before the natives ever saw a pair of scissors.

Evolution of the Myth

We have all heard the stories about the great danger in dangling a finger into water inhabited by piranhas, about a foolish bather being reduced to a skeleton in a matter of minutes, and ranchers having to sacrifice a cow to appease the piranhas' savage hunger before driving their cattle across a piranha-infested river.

Among the earliest accounts of piranhas to reach Europe were those of George Margrave's 1648 publication, *Historia Naturalis Brasiliae*. All the elements of horror so prominent in later tales are present, including their sharp teeth and savage nature, the danger of entering piranha-infested waters, and their ability to cleanly bite off chunks of flesh. Alexander Von Humboldt, in his early-1800s narratives document-

ing his South American travels, stressed their vicious nature, referring to them as one of the continent's greatest scourges.

Famous later accounts were the writings of no less eminent a person than Theodore Roosevelt, the explorer, hunter, soldier, and 26th president of the United States. Included in his sensationalized tales of the piranha's ferocity is one of a rider who fell from his horse when fording a stream being quickly reduced to a skeleton. There is no mention about why the horse wasn't attacked too!

Even reputable modern writers disagree when it comes to piranhas. The anthropologist Harold Schultz, after spending more than two decades traveling widely through Brazil, flatly states: "In all these years I have never had a harmful experience with these greatly feared piranhas." On the other hand, the great ichthyologist George Myers was a bit more cautious. In *The Piranha Book* (see Information) he writes that four

species are always dangerous to man and then describes the piranhas that are now included within the genus *Pygocentrus*.

Seeking the Truth

Any traveler to regions of South America inhabited by piranhas will routinely observe children swimming and splashing about in the water while their mothers are doing the wash nearby. Men are frequently seen almost completely submerged, pulling fish seines and setting gill nets. No one seems the least bit concerned about the potential for piranha attacks. I have also commonly seen domestic cattle wading in shallows and ducks, iguanas, and snakes swimming across

The local people are not fearful of being attacked by piranhas while in the water. Adults and children eagerly volunteer to help us in our fish collecting efforts.

rivers, all totally unmolested. In my numerous trips to Amazonian Brazil and Peru to do research or lead tropical fish–collecting ecotours, there has never been a single incident of anyone being attacked by piranhas while in the water. I consider this significant because we spend so much time pulling seines, setting fish traps, and swimming or fording rivers and streams, including those inhabited by large numbers of the supposedly dangerous red-bellied piranha, *Pygocentrus nattereri*. As a matter of fact, the only piranha bites were the result of someone carelessly removing a piranha from a fishhook or taking one out of a net.

I have frequently asked local people whether they fear piranhas. The most common response is that the most dangerous piranha is one flopping about in the bottom of their dugout canoe. They often dramatize their story by curling one of their toes under their foot to simulate a piranha amputation. Ivan Sazima (see Information) wrote that many of the reports of piranhas cannibalizing people were actually the result of the fish scavenging the corpses of people who had died from drowning.

Would I therefore consider piranhas totally harmless to humans? I wouldn't go that far. All the piranha stories cannot be totally dismissed. We must also realize that only a very few species, all within the genus *Pygocentrus*, have the potential of being dangerous to humans and that the sharpness of their dentition and strength of their jaws is a frightening reality. In

In parts of Venezuela, Pygocentrus cariba *is known as the* capaburro *(donkey castrator).*

some parts of Venezuela piranhas have earned the unsavory reputation of attacking the udders and male genitalia of cattle, earning *Pygocentrus cariba* the local name of *capaburro*, or donkey castrator. Piranhas are also known to be potentially dangerous below rookeries of waterbirds where they wait for fledglings and other food items to fall from the nests. They become so conditioned to this food source that anything that hits the water with a splash—such as someone falling from a canoe—has the potential of being attacked. Several horrific cases of piranha attacks have been reported in recent years after someone has accidentally fallen into the water from a dock where fishermen routinely clean their catch and throw the refuse back into the river. In such situations piranhas become habituated to this food source and eagerly attack anything that appears to have been dumped into the water, be it fish offal or a human being.

One thing that cannot be refuted is that in South America piranhas of all kinds are considered a popular food fish and that many more piranhas are eaten by humans than the other way around.

A Special Note About Photographs

Many of the photographs used in this book were taken by biologists and collectors in the field immediately after capture, using a field photo tank or by simply laying the specimen down on a suitable substrate. While these images are less aesthetically pleasing than those taken in a well-planted aquarium, they are the best means of conveying the true colors and body weight of piranhas in nature. Wherever possible important locale data is provided.

It is risky to attempt the identification of many piranhas from photographs alone, but I have taken great pains to be as accurate as possible. I have clearly indicated where either the true nature of a species is still in doubt or the identification of the specimen illustrated is tentative or uncertain.

PIRANHA TAXONOMY AND ANATOMY

It sometimes becomes necessary to change a species' scientific name. This may be because of our increasing knowledge about its relationship or because it becomes apparent that it had been previously described under a different name. These changes can be frustrating to biologists and hobbyists alike, but still must be done.

Taxonomy

Taxonomy is the science of identifying, describing, classifying, and naming living organisms. Every described species is given a scientific name consisting of two italicized words written in Latin or in a Latinized form. The first word is called the *generic name* and is always capitalized. The second part of the name is the *species* and never capitalized. Sometimes a species is further divided into *subspecies* or geographic variants.

This **Serrasalmus serrulatus** *(upper) and* **Pygopristis denticulata** *(lower) show how similar different species of piranhas can appear, even those from two different genera. This is a major factor contributing to misidentification of species. Both these fish were caught in the blackwater Rio Nanay outside of Iquitos, Peru.*

At times, not every authority agrees with the validity of a described species, but taxonomy, as with all science, is constantly evolving.

Several ichthyologists and field biologists are presently working with some of the more challenging species. This involves collecting large numbers of specimens from as wide an area as possible, then carefully comparing them with each other, the original descriptions, and type specimens (if these important specimens still exist). Molecular biological studies of many of these fishes are already being done. This is all difficult, expensive, and time-consuming work, but it is hoped that it will lead to a more accurate understanding of these fish.

Classification

Piranhas are described as characoid fish belonging to the subfamily Serrasalminae,

This piranha from the Rio Negro is usually identified by Brazilian fish exporters as **Serrasalmus eigenmanni,** *but this is probably an incorrect name for a species that requires much further study.*

within the family Characidae. Almost all characoid fish have teeth, scales, and an adipose fin, and lack a spiny portion to dorsal and adipose fins, but some uniquely evolved species may lack one or more of these structures. Characoids, together with the silurids (catfishes) and cyprinids (minnows), are referred to as *ostariophysan* fishes. This refers to a series of modified

The sawlike modified ventral scales called **serrae** *are a characteristic of all fish in the subfamily Serrasalminae. This is a* **Serrasalmus elongatus. Rio Orosa, Peru.**

vertebrae that connects the swim bladder with the internal ear. This structure is called the Weberian apparatus and greatly enhances their hearing of high-frequency sounds. The skin of characoid fishes has the ability to secrete chemical alarm signals in the form of pheromones that can elicit a fright reaction in others of the same species.

The subfamily Serrasalminae is recognized by the presence of a unique combination of characteristics not found in other characins. The name *Serrasalminae*, meaning "salmon with a saw," refers to the characteristic ventral keel of saw-toothed, modified scales called *serrae* found in all species within this taxonomic unit. The number and shape of the serrae may vary among the different species and is one of the anatomic characteristics used in separating them. Serrasalmins also have numerous small scales and are rather deep bodied and laterally compressed; some are almost disc-shaped. In addition to piranhas, this subfamily includes the various pacus and silver dollars of the generally accepted genera *Acnodon, Catoprion, Colossoma, Metynnis, Myleus, Mylesinus, Mylossoma, Piaractus,* and the more uncertain genera *Tometes* and *Utiaritichthys.*

An important taxonomic feature long used in separating the true piranhas from their serrasalmin relatives is their teeth. Typically, piranha teeth are three-cusped with the center cusp distinctly triangular in shape, sharp-edged and much larger than the two lateral ones. In each jaw these razor-sharp teeth are arranged in a single row. On each tooth one of the small lateral cusps fits tightly into a recess in the adjoining tooth, effectively securing together all the teeth in each half of a jaw into a single, rigid, functional unit. The teeth of non-piranha

This skull of a **Pygocentrus cariba** *clearly shows the typical piranha dentition.*

Genus *Pygopristis*

This is a monotypic (containing only one species) genus with the five-cusped piranha, *P. denticulata*, being the single recognized species. The musculature and anatomy of its jaws are weaker than in other piranhas, and

Pygopristis denticulata *is the only species within its genus. Rio Atabaso near junction with Rio Orinoco, Venezuela.*

serrasalmins are noninterlocking and frequently arranged in a double row. Two exceptions are the five-cusped piranha, *Pygopristis denticulata*, and the wimpel piranha, *Catoprion mento*. As can be assumed from its name, the teeth of the five-cusped piranha are multi-cusped, whereas those of the strange wimpel piranha are not arranged in single interlocking rows. Readers who are surprised at the inclusion of the wimpel piranha within the true piranhas are referred to the genus discussion page 16.

Piranha Genera

Most modern authorities have divided the true piranhas into four genera—*Pygopristis, Serrasalmus, Pristobrycon,* and *Pygocentrus*—but new research is suggesting that major changes might be indicated in the placement of the monotypic genus *Catoprion* and within the genus *Pristobrycon* (see the following discussion of these two genera). There are even some biologists who think the serrasalmins should be elevated to full family rank.

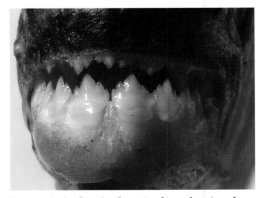

Pygopristis denticulata *is the only piranha to have small secondary cusps on its teeth. This is responsible for its common name of "five-cusped piranha."*

Pristobrycon calmoni *is the type species of its genus.*

its relatively small but interlocking teeth have five rounded cusps instead of the one large triangular cusp flanked by two small ones. For these and other anatomic reasons *P. denticulata* is thought to be the most primitive of the piranhas and the one least adapted to a truly predatory lifestyle. In nature it feeds mainly on seeds and fruit, plus some fish fins and flesh. Unlike all other known piranhas this species is sexually dimorphic, the outer margin of the male's anal fin being lobed rather than straight.

Genus *Pristobrycon*

This is a problematic genus closely related to *Serrasalmus*. Pristobrycons tend to be deep bodied, with some nearly disclike in shape. Their jaws and teeth are weaker than those of *Serrasalmus* or *Pygocentrus*, and there are usually a few blunt teeth on the roof of their mouths (ectopterygoid teeth) that may or may not be lost with maturity. These are the piranhas sometimes referred to as *pirambebas* in the literature.

Pristobrycon was established by Carl H. Eigenmann in 1915 to accommodate the species *P. calmoni*, known at the time as *Pygocentrus calmoni*. Since that date several other species have been described as belonging to this genus. The validity of a few of them has been questioned, and others have been moved to the genus *Serrasalmus* (see *Serrasalmus eigenmanni, serrulatus, humeralis, hollandi,* and *scapularis*). There have also been suggestions to synonymize this genus with *Serrasalmus* or place it as a subgenus under it. Most controversial are two separate 2007 publications by Hubert et al. and Freeman et al. Using both detailed anatomic studies and molecular biology they suggested that *P. striolatus* is not a *pristobrycon*, that it should be moved into a new genus with it as the type species, and that it is most closely related to *Pygopristis denticulata* and *Catoprion mento*! The jury is still out on these suggestions, and at present the following five species are still usually included within the genus: *Pristobrycon* aureus, *P. calmoni*, *P. maculipinnis*, *P. striolatus*, and *P. careospinus*. It is interesting to note that *Pristobrycon careospinus* was described in 1992 from one specimen and hasn't been seen since.

Genus *Serrasalmus*

This was the first described genus of piranhas, being erected in 1766 for *Salmo (Serrasalmus) rhombeus*. Since then piranhas have been divided into four separate genera, but *Serrasalmus* still contains the vast majority of species, with about 25 considered valid and definitely more to come. They vary in shape from almost discoid to quite elongate, with most being moderately deep-bodied and more or less diamond shaped. All have a preanal spine. It is probable that several species, such as *S. rhombeus* and *S. eigenmanni* will turn out to be complexes of several distinct species of similar appearance.

Mitochondria DNA sequencing has shown this genus to be monophyletic. These piranhas have powerful to very powerful jaws and well-developed, razor-sharp teeth. There are also usually eight to ten well-developed teeth on the palate, although these may be more or less lost in some species (particularly those previously placed in the genus *Pristobrycon*) with maturity. The dorsal contour of the head and nape is convex, easily separating this genus from *Pygocentrus* (see below). Some *Serrasalmus* piranhas, such as *S. rhombeus* and *S. manueli*, are reported to reach the impressive size of almost 2 feet (60 cm) and a weight of 5 pounds (2.2 kg).

The majority of these piranhas feed heavily on fish fins when young, gradually changing to a diet of whole small fish and chunks of fish flesh with maturity. Plants, seeds, and fruit may

This subadult black piranha is typical of its genus. Rio Tigre near junction with Rio Marañon, Peru.

be seasonally important dietary components of many species. In nature they tend to be solitary, but some, such as *S. rhombeus* and *S. sanchezi*, appear to sometimes form loosely organized groups.

Genus *Pygocentrus*

This genus comprises three known species. They are the piranhas of myth and legend, and all are listed as potentially dangerous to humans. All three are covered in more detail later in this book.

A convex, rather than concave, dorsal profile of the head and nape region easily separates them from all other piranha species. This characteristic is obvious in fish as small as 1 inch (2.5 cm). Their heads and jaws are also wider and more powerfully built than those of any

Taddyella and *Rooseveltiella*, both honoring Theodore (Teddy) Roosevelt, are previous names that have applied to the genus *Pygocentrus*.

This yellow form of **Pygocentrus piraya** *shows the convex shape of the head and nape region typical of this genus.*

other genus of piranhas, and their palate is never toothed.

Genus *Catoprion*

This monotypic genus contains only one species, *Catoprion mento*, the wimpel (usually mispelled "wimple") piranha. Despite the word *piranha* in its common name, this fish has historically never been considered a true piranha. For one thing, this scale-eating fish lacks the

*Until recently, the wimpel piranha, **Catoprion mento**, was not considered a true piranha. New evidence indicates that it actually belongs within this group.*

interlocking, triangular teeth that have been considered the hallmark of all true piranhas. Although the recently deceased characin authority Jacques Géry placed it in a subfamily of its own, most ichthyologists considered it a serrasalmin related to, but in a different evolutionary lineage from, the true piranhas.

It now looks like these opinions might have to be drastically changed. The two studies mentioned previously (see the genus *Pristobrycon*, above) suggest that *Catoprion* forms a natural evolutionary grouping with *Pygopristis denticulata* and *Pristobrycon striolatus*. Therefore, if we consider *Pygopristis denticulata* and *Pristobrycon striolatus* piranhas, then we must include *Catoprion* too. If further research bears this out, the wimpel piranha would be considered a highly specialized species of piranha and not a piranha relative (and *P. striolatus* would have to be removed from the genus *Pristobrycon*).

Piranha Senses

Hearing: Because of the Weberian apparatus (see Classification, above), piranhas have excellent hearing. An organ within their skulls called the *labyrinth* contains the inner ear as well as an organ that controls balance.

Smell: Experiments have shown that piranhas have an acute sense of smell that undoubtedly aids them in finding food in the frequently murky waters they inhabit. The paired nostrils are on the dorsal surface of the head between the eyes and upper jaw. Each nostril consists of two openings separated by a flap of skin. Water entering the nostrils flows over a highly sensitive and much folded olfactory membrane.

Vision: Piranhas' eyes are on the sides of their heads, providing a very wide lateral

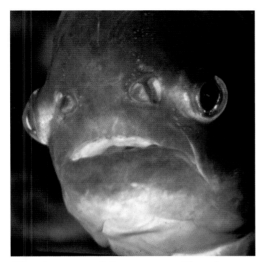

The placement of the eyes as well as the flap that divides each nostril in half are shown in this portrait of a red-bellied piranha.

The lateral line is particularly prominent on this juvenile **Serrasalmus serrulatus.** *Rio Nanay, Peru.*

expanse of vision but a limited anterior stereoscopic field. They are best adapted for seeing in daylight, but the retina may also possess a reflective layer that enhances nighttime vision. Piranhas have excellent color vision, and tests indicate that they are able to perceive infrared wavelengths invisible to humans.

Taste: The taste buds of piranhas are concentrated within their mouth and pharynx, with a lesser number on their lips. In general, fish are not supposed to have a particularly well-developed sense of taste, but we have all seen them quickly spit out a potential food item that is not to their liking.

Lateral line: The lateral line is a sensory organ found only in fish. In piranhas it can be clearly observed as a thin line of small pores on the mid-side of the body extending from behind the gill plate to the base of the tail. Sensory cells, called *neuromasts*, under the scales of the lateral line, detect vibrations coming through the water as well as the direction of water currents. By detecting the reflected pressure waves produced when the piranha approaches a submerged object, this organ is an important navigational aid. It is also sensitive enough to respond to the vibrations created by a swimming or struggling fish.

PIRANHAS IN NATURE

Contrary to popular opinion, the waters of the Amazon and other major South American rivers are not invariably very soft and acidic. As a matter of fact, the main channel of the Amazon generally has a pH close to neutral and is only moderately soft (80–120 ppm total hardness).

Distribution

Piranhas are native only to the tropical and subtropical regions of South America east of the Andes Mountains. The Amazon is the mightiest river of the region, flowing more than 4,000 miles (6,400 km) from its source in the high Andes of Peru to its mouth on the Atlantic coast of Brazil. It is the largest river on Earth and contains approximately 20 percent of the world's fresh water. Oceangoing vessels are able to navigate more than 2,300 miles (3,703 km) upriver to Iquitos, the farthest-inland port city in the world.

The Amazon's largest tributary is the famed Rio Negro of Brazil. Within the Guiana Highlands the Brazo Casiquiare connects the headwaters of the Rio Negro with those of the

The junction of the Rio Tacshacuraray with the Rio Napo, Peru. Several species of piranhas can be found here.

Orinoco. This Venezuelan river (with tributaries also originating in Colombia) is home to at least 15 species of piranhas, some endemic to this river system but others also found within the Amazon. Various other species are found in the smaller rivers and streams of the Guianas and Suriname east of the Orinoco.

Another major South American river that is inhabited with piranhas is the São Francisco of

Note: Brazil refers to that portion of the Amazon River upstream from the confluence of the Rio Negro by the name of Rio Solimoes, and many maps list both names. This book will follow the more common practice of considering the Amazon River proper to start at the confluence of the Marañon and Ucayali Rivers in northern Peru. The actual source of the Amazon is a spring high up in the Andes Mountains of Peru.

The shorelines and floodplains of whitewater rivers are composed of thick layers of mud formed by the deposition of suspended silt. Rio Momon outside of Iquitos, Peru.

eastern Brazil. So far only two piranha species have been described from here, *Serrasalmus brandi* and *Pygocentrus piraya*. More southern rivers that support populations of piranhas are the Paraná and Paraguay that drain southern Brazil, Paraguay, northeastern Argentina, and Uruguay. Winter cold limits the existence of piranhas here and large winter kills of red-bellied piranhas are regularly reported from middle and lower reaches of the Paraguay River south of Asunción, Paraguay.

The Water

South American waters inhabited by piranhas can be classified into three distinct types—whitewater, blackwater, and clearwater. Each has its own unique set of characteristics related to its source, but these become blurred and less clear where waters of different types meet and mix. Many species of fish, including piranhas,

prefer or are limited to a certain water type. This is particularly true for blackwater forms. Knowing where a species of fish comes from can be important for successfully maintaining and breeding them in captivity.

Whitewater

The main channel of the Amazon and other rivers that originate in the Andes Mountains are categorized as whitewater. They carry an enormous load of suspended silt that is responsible for their turbidity and muddy-brown (not white) color. Although relatively rich in nutrients, the opacity prevents the growth of submerged aquatic vegetation. The shoreline, bottom, and floodplains of whitewater rivers are made up of thick layers of fine mud continually being deposited as the suspended silt settles to the bottom. Characteristic of whitewater rivers is the extensive development of floating plant communities and the presence of dense growths of shoreline reeds.

These waters are only moderately soft and close to neutral in pH. Depending on the season, my numerous tests of Amazon River water near the Peruvian city of Iquitos showed a total hardness varying between 80 and 120 ppm (parts per million), and a pH between 6.8 and 7.3. Whitewater, being the most nutrient rich of the three water types, is the most biologically productive with the greatest numbers and species of fish (including piranhas).

Because of the nutrient-rich muds deposited by whitewater rivers their floodplains are the only truly rich soils in the Amazon basin. This, combined with their accessibility, has resulted in large areas having been cleared for logging, the expansion of villages, and farming. The effect of these operations on the multitudes of

The different appearance of whitewater and blackwater is clearly seen here at the junction of the blackwater Rio Nanay with the whitewater Amazon outside of Iquitos, Peru.

Blackwaters are very soft and quite acidic. Their deep brown color is caused by the abundance of tannins. Uracoa Morichales, Venezuela.

aquatic and terrestrial species dependent upon this habitat is still being studied.

Blackwater

Rivers and streams originating in swamps and forest lowlands carry minimal amounts of suspended matter. The water is transparent, but stained a deep brown color from the tannins produced by the decay of leaves and other vegetation. The shorelines of blackwater rivers are either sandy or claylike, lacking the muddy silt deposits of whitewater floodplains. Blackwater rivers and streams are generally quite sterile, very poor in nutrients, extremely soft, and moderately to strongly acidic. Although their pH is generally in the 5.0–6.0 range, readings as low as 3.2–4.5 are not unheard of. The most famous of the blackwater rivers is Brazil's Rio Negro (Negro meaning "black"). It is also the largest tributary of the Amazon, with a water flow exceeding the second-largest river in the world, Africa's Zaire (formerly Congo). Because of these rivers' low productivity the foods for nonpredatory blackwater fish frequently come from sources outside the river, such as terrestrial insects, seeds, and fruit.

Many Amazonian fish, including piranhas, time their breeding season to coincide with the beginning of the rise in water levels and its associated abundance of food.

The Rio Iriri of central Brazil is a fast flowing clearwater river.

Clearwater

Clearwater rivers originate in geologically old and highly eroded uplands, such as the Brazilian and Guiana Highlands. They lack the dissolved tannins of blackwater and are silt free. Their waters are frequently so transparent that the refraction of light often makes them appear to be tinted a slight green or blue. Because of their clarity the sun can penetrate deeply, often resulting in a rich and diverse population of submerged aquatic vegetation. The pH of clearwater is variable, but usually somewhere between 6.0 and neutral. Clearwater supports a diverse fish fauna, with small species being particularly abundant. Here they find food and shelter among the submerged vegetation and tree roots. Typical clearwater rivers are the Xingu, Tapajos, and Tocantins.

Seasonal Changes

Rainfall in the Amazon basin averages between 60 and 120 inches (150–300 cm) annually, but does not fall uniformly throughout the year. The year can be divided into two seasons, wet and less wet. This, combined with the seasonal precipitation in the Andes and other highland regions, and summer snow melt on the higher peaks, results in great fluctuations of water levels. The larger rivers may undergo a seasonal rise and fall of 20 to more than 50 feet (6.1–17.5 m). Because of this, seasonally inundated floodplain forests are characteristic of the region. As the waters rise, they overflow their banks and flood the forest for many miles inland. Fish enter what was formerly dry-land forests

The high water mark on the large banyan tree dramatically indicates how high the water rose during the previous wet season. Peruvian Amazon.

and savannahs. Swimming among the trunks of trees, they feed voraciously on new food sources that include forest insects, fallen fruits, seeds, and nutritious detritus. This seasonal food source is particularly important for fish that inhabit the nonproductive black waters.

Natural Behavior and Diet

Behavior

Depending upon species, season, abundance of food, and age class, piranhas may be solitary, travel in small, loosely organized groups, or travel in large shoals. Those living in groups tend not to form well-organized schools, but rather loosely organized assemblages in which each fish maintains its own personal space. Observations indicate that piranhas are particularly edgy when approached from the rear—possibly as a precaution against fin-eating piranha attacks. In general, the scale feeders tend to be solitary hunters, whereas the red-bellies of genus *Pygocentrus* are usually found in shoals.

It is known that some species, such as *S. rhombeus*, may hunt at night, but the majority are most active during the daylight hours.

It has been theorized by Dr. Kirk Winemiller (see References) that the false eyespots at the base of the tail found in many species of Amazonian fish cause the tail region to resemble a head, thus confusing piranhas planning an attack. This may explain the proportionately less piranha-caused fin damage seen in fish with these caudal eyespots compared with fishes of similar size and habitat preferences that lack these markings.

The hunting activities of the larger predatory species apparently peak during the hours of dawn and dusk, with the midday being spent resting in sheltered areas. From these retreats one or two individuals may launch an attack upon passing prey. Foraging by other species and young individuals seems to be more evenly distributed throughout the day. At night, piranhas have been observed resting quietly among plant roots and submerged logs and branches. I have never caught a piranha of any species on hook and line when fishing at night.

Diet

The common perception is that all piranhas are voracious, obligate, flesh-eating carnivores, but many scientific studies of piranhas in the wild plus analysis of stomach contents have shown this view to be erroneous. The diets of many species have yet to be fully studied, but it is becoming increasingly clear that most piranhas are opportunistic omnivores with their diets varying not only according to food abundance, age, and species, but also by genera. This might help explain why in most regions many different piranha species often coexist. With each exploiting a different food source direct competition is minimized.

Juvenile piranhas less than $4/5$ of an inch (20 mm) in length feed mainly upon planktonic organisms and microcrustacea, adding aquatic insect larvae to their diet as they grow. By the time they have reached $1\frac{1}{2}$ inches (3.75 cm), most have switched to a diet heavily composed of fish fins and the flesh of small fish. Fins are an abundant, nutritious, and renewable food source. *Pygocentrus* piranhas are an exception in that they omit the fin-eating stage and progress directly to fish flesh and whole small fish.

This juvenile black piranha (right) has just bitten off a portion from the tail of a silver tetra,
Tetragonopterus argenteus.

With approaching maturity, differences in food preferences among the various genera become more pronounced. The short-faced and comparatively weak-jawed *Pristobrycon* and *Pygopristis* species are truly omnivorous, feeding on seeds, fruit, leaves, and other vegetable matter plus fish fins, scales and flesh, including that of other piranhas. It is interesting to note that whereas the fins, scales, and flesh are swallowed without first being chewed, the seeds are first thoroughly masticated into tiny bits.

As would be expected from a genus as diverse as *Serrasalmus*, dietary preferences vary among the different species. The elongate piranha, *S. elongatus* and *S. irritans,* specialize in the fins of other fish, whereas larger species such as the black piranha, *S. rhombeus*, and Manuel's piranha, *S. manueli*, feed mainly upon fish flesh and entire other fish. Piranhas of all species are also efficient scavengers, raiding gill nets and quickly devouring the carcasses of any species (even human!) they encounter. I have personally observed large numbers of red-bellied piranhas in the Rio Orosa of Peru feeding upon the bodies of fish killed by temporarily low dissolved oxygen levels.

It has long been known that because of the increased time needed to digest plant material vegetarian species of animals have longer intestinal tracts than carnivores. Studies by Dr. Leo Nico have shown that the intestinal lengths of various Venezuelan piranhas correlate well with their diets.

Hunting methods: Underwater observations by biologists of piranhas in the Pantenal region of Brazil have discovered that piranhas use a variety of hunting strategies. These include techniques of ambush, stalking, active chases, and approaching under guise. Although the first three are self-explanatory, the last is worth explaining in more detail. *Serrasalmus spilopleura* have been observed openly lingering in full view of their intended prey without showing any overt interest in them. Ever so slowly they edge closer so as not to cause any alarm. Only at the very last minute do they dash forward to clip off a piece of fin or a bite of flesh.

Aggressive mimicry: The young of many piranhas up to a size of 2 inches (5 cm) are plain silver with a black spot at the base of the tail. At this stage they closely resemble many other characins of similar size, such as various species

of *Astyanax, Moenkhausia, Poptella,* and
Tetragonopterus. It has been proposed that this
might be a type of aggressive mimicry. At this
size many piranhas feed heavily on fins; being
able to inconspicuously mingle with their potential food source has great survival advantages.

Cleaning: A rather recently reported finding
is that *Serrasalmus marginatus* may under
some circumstances act as a cleaner species,
removing external parasites such as fish lice
and anchor worms from the bodies of other
piranhas. The marine environment has many
species of cleaner fish, but this behavior in
freshwater fish has rarely been reported.

**Defense strategies of other fish species
against piranhas:** As can be expected, other
fish have developed several lines of defense
against piranha attacks. Many reflect the piranhas' habits of approaching intended prey from
the rear and directing their main attack at the
tail region. It is known that several cichlid
species when approached by piranhas will
gather themselves into a defensive ring with
their tails to the center. Some of the larger
cichlids, and characins such as the so-called
freshwater barracudas (characin genus *Acestro-
ryhchus*), may actually repel piranhas with
frontal attacks and aggressive displays.

Piranha Reproduction

The reproduction of most piranha species has
not been observed in nature nor achieved in
captivity. The limited firsthand observations of
actual piranha reproduction in the wild, combined with findings of when small young have
been caught, indicate that piranhas start to
breed at the onset of the rainy season when the
water levels first begin to rise. The fry then seek

Much of the diet of **Pristobrycon striolatus** *is
comprised of masticated seeds.*

areas of floating vegetation or flooded mead-
ows where their foods are abundant. The local
peoples have long insisted that these fish pre-
pare nests and guard their eggs, a behavior
later confirmed in aquarium spawnings of several species of *Serrasalmus* and *Pygocentrus.*
What is not yet known is if piranhas of all piranha genera practice such an advanced reproductive mode or if some simply scatter their
eggs, as do most of their serrasalmin relatives.

One of the main reasons there are so few
records of piranhas breeding in captivity is the

Serrasalmus marginatus *has been observed
in nature cleaning parasites from the body
and fins of other species of piranhas.*

Piranhas prefer to approach their prey from the rear. The false eyespot at the base of this Oscar's (Astronotus ocellatus) tail is thought to deter attacks by causing the tail end to resemble a head.

highly aggressive behavior of most toward con-specifics. Attempted pairings often result in mutilation or death of one or both of the fish rather than reproduction. It is known that the coloration of many species of piranhas in breed-ing condition darkens considerably, often obscur-ing much of their body markings. Aquarium observations of successful spawnings indicate that a male piranha often selects and defends a breeding site among submerged natural or artifi-cial vegetation, plant roots, or a similar artificial

At present, no piranha species is considered threatened or severely declining in numbers.

substrate and then initiates courtship by actively pursuing a female. Most pairs then create a depression in the substrate or remove excess vegetation from the breeding site by biting it off with their teeth. A bowl-like hollow is soon created in which they lay their eggs. Spawning is a protracted affair and may take several hours to complete. Depending on the size and species of the breeding pair, several hundred to several thousand eggs approximately $^1/_8$ inch (3.2 mm) in diameter are produced. One or both parents vigorously defend the nest territory against other fish of moderate to large size, but small fish such as neon tetras (*Parachierodon innesi*) are not harmed, even when they enter the nest to devour the eggs. This surprising observation has been seen in both nature and captive spawnings.

Hatching time varies from two to five days, depending upon water temperature and possi-bly the species. The fry become free-swimming after several more days, then leave the nest and seek food and shelter among submerged and floating vegetation. The roots of floating water

The colors of many piranhas darken during the breeding season. Compare the nonbreeding Sanchez's piranha (left) with the one in breeding coloration (right). Rio Orosa, Peru.

hyacinth, *Echhornia crassipes*, and water lettuce, *Pistia stratiotes* (both native to the Amazon region) appear to be particularly attractive to piranha fry less than $1/2$ inch (1 cm) in length. Although in captivity most piranhas grow quite slowly, studies of fish caught in the wild indicate that under natural conditions many species become sexually mature in less than two years, well before they are fully grown. Several observations of red-bellied piranhas breeding in the wild indicate that they may at times be gregarious spawners, with many pairs nesting in close proximity. This behavior is very reminiscent of the North American sunfishes of the family Centrarchidae.

Natural Enemies

Adult piranhas have few natural enemies. Many are too large to be of interest to most fish-eating birds such as herons and cormorants and are given a wide berth by most diurnal predatory fish. A small number are undoubtedly taken by caimans (South American crocodilians), fish eagles, and the increasingly rare giant river otters. This probably peaks in the dry season when large numbers of piranhas are frequently isolated in drying floodplain lakes, where they provide easy pickings. It has been frequently stated in the literature that possibly the major natural predator of piranhas are the two species of freshwater Amazonian dolphins, and that the larger of the two, known as the pink porpoise, or *boto* (*Inia geoffrensis*), has a particular taste for piranha flesh. Other probable predators of importance are the many species of large to enormous catfish that inhabit the same rivers as piranhas. Young piranhas are fair game for many species of waterbirds, aquatic reptiles, and

Large numbers of piranhas are caught for food. The larger silvery fish are **Prochilodus nigricans.**

predatory fishes. They are also preyed upon by larger piranhas.

The seasonal rise and fall of most waters where piranhas live is also directly and indirectly responsible for numerous piranha deaths. During the dry season many piranhas of all sizes become trapped in desiccating floodplain lakes and ponds cut off from the rivers. Most either die or become food items for predators and scavengers such as fish-eating mammals, wading birds, water snakes, and vultures.

Although this might be surprising to some, humans are undoubtedly one of the major predators of adult piranhas. Throughout their range, piranhas are considered a desirable food fish, and huge numbers are caught in nets and on hook-and-line. Many are sold by local fishermen in the ubiquitous outdoor markets.

Three major criteria to consider when purchasing an aquarium for your piranhas are its shape, size, and construction.

Selecting the Aquarium

Shape and size: Aquariums generally come in three major styles based on their proportions—*standard* (which includes bow-front models), *long*, and *high*. While the high type might be attractive and require little floor space, it is totally unsuitable for fish like piranhas that prefer room for horizontal swimming and the establishment of territories based on square inches of bottom space. They also provide very little surface area for gas exchange.

When selecting an aquarium, always take into consideration the adult size and behavior of the fish species you are intending to keep. Obviously, larger fish require more room, but with piranhas behavioral traits are just as important. Piranhas are not considered

A shoal of red-bellied piranhas share their large aquarium with a school of cardinal tetras, **Paracheirodon axelrodi.**

particularly active fish, but as aquarium fish go, most grow to a large or very large size, are nervous, and are prone to repeatedly rubbing their mouths against the glass when kept in an aquarium that is too small for their comfort level. Those species that are considered more or less amenable to being kept together in small groups can without warning become highly territorial and persecute or mutilate each other, particularly when not given enough room. I would recommend that you house your piranha in an aquarium of standard or long design. I consider 50 gallons (190 L) the minimum capacity for maintaining a single specimen of most of the medium- to larger-size piranhas. Single specimens of a few of the smaller piranhas or young specimens of other varieties can be housed in proportionately smaller quarters. One should never attempt to keep adult specimens of the really large piranhas, such as *Serrasalmus rhombeus* and *Pygocentrus piraya,*

A well-maintained aquarium can be an attractive part of any room. This one is 55 gallons (207 L) and standard shape.

aquarium plus its water and furnishings (see Weight, below). Most commercially available aquarium stands are of either wrought iron or wooden construction. Wrought-iron stands are inexpensive but not particularly attractive. Wooden stands can be very attractive and also provide cabinet space for storage and hiding filters and electric outlets. Some of the better wooden stands are of furniture quality and finished with a water-resistant coating. Where appearance is not important, you can easily build your own stand out of Haydite construction blocks and pressure-treated four-by-four lumber.

or small shoals of species the size of *Pygocentrus nattereri* and *Sererasalmus geryi* in anything less than 200 gallons (760 L).

Aquarium construction: Almost all aquariums being manufactured today are of frameless "all-glass" or acrylic construction. Most glass aquariums have their five panes held together with silicone adhesive, but recently glass aquariums made in one molded piece have appeared on the market. Acrylic aquariums are also of molded construction with a top brace sometimes added after the molding process and attached by a chemical bond. The advantages of molded glass or acrylic aquariums are that there are no seams to possibly split and leak. Acrylic aquariums are also considerably lighter than glass aquariums of the same gallonage, and where weight is an important consideration they might be the best choice. Disadvantages are their usually higher price and scratchability.

Aquarium stands: The single most important thing to consider when buying or building an aquarium stand is that it be constructed strongly enough to safely support the weight of the

Aquarium Placement

Some factors to be taken into consideration when selecting a location for your aquarium are natural light levels, weight, and proximity to utilities.

Light levels: Unless you first place an opaque backing on your aquarium it is best not to locate it in front of a window. Not only will the daylight shining through the fish prevent you from observing their beautiful colors, but it can also cause the aquarium to overheat and encourage excess growths of algae.

Weight: One gallon (3.8 L) of water weighs 8.33 pounds (3.6 kg). A fully set-up 50-gallon (190 L), all-glass aquarium complete with gravel, rocks, and water weighs at least 600 pounds (270 kg). Larger aquariums are proportionately heavier. This makes it obvious that you need to give careful thought to the placement of your aquarium. The floors of many homes and apartment houses are not built to support such a massive and concentrated weight. Ground-level or basement floors are generally stronger than those of upper levels, and many buildings limit the size of aquariums permitted on upper floors. If you plan to purchase an unusually large aquarium, and the foundation of your home is anything other than concrete slab construction, it is prudent to first consult a structural engineer.

Utilities: An aquarium requires the use of lights, heaters, pumps, motors, and water. For convenience, it is essential that you locate your aquarium near electrical outlets. If you are able to place the aquarium stand in front of such an outlet, all wires and extension cords will be hidden. Because aquarium maintenance will require periodic siphoning of debris and partial water changes, try to locate it within siphon-hose distance of a sink.

Aquarium Equipment

Lights: Depending upon style, aquarium light fixtures can be included as part of a full aquarium hood or can be a separate unit (strip light) that rests either on the frame of the aquarium or the glass aquarium cover.

Unless you intend to house your piranhas in an aquarium with living plants, the main purpose of an aquarium light will be to provide enough light of the proper spectrum to satisfactorily view your fish. I recommend standard fluorescent aquarium fixtures fitted with bulbs of a "daylight" spectrum. "Cool white" bulbs tend to give your fish a washed-out appearance, and "plant-gro" tubes distort the fish's colors. For those interested in attempting to set up a planted aquarium for their piranhas there

An accurate thermometer is essential for monitoring your aquarium's water temperature.

are many excellent high-output light fixtures available. These use either HO (high output), VHO (very high output), metal halide bulbs, or some combination of these.

Heaters and thermometers: Most piranhas prefer water temperatures between 75 and 80°F (24–27°C), and in most homes and fish rooms a thermostatically controlled aquarium heater is required to maintain this temperature range. Heaters come in two basic styles: those that are suspended in the water by a clamp that attaches to the aquarium's top margin, and those that are fully submersible. Submersible heaters are particularly suitable for homes with young children who might become tempted to turn the temperature adjustment knob on a hang-on heater. Whichever type you decide to use, the rule of thumb is that you should provide three watts per gallon (one W per 1.25 L). A 50-gallon (190 L) aquarium would therefore require a 150-watt heater. Instead of using one heater of the proper wattage, some aquarists prefer to use two units, each providing half of the required output. This slows the overheating of the water if a heater's thermostat gets stuck in the "on" position, and would also slow the chilling if one heater should stop functioning.

Air pumps: An air pump can be used to run air-driven filters as well as airstones. Many aquarists do not realize that an air pump is not always needed. If their filters are not air-driven and produce adequate water circulation essential for surface gas exchange, there is no need for additional airstones.

Most of the commonly sold air pumps are of the vibrator type where a vibrating rubber diaphragm produces a flow of air. These pumps are available in many sizes. Some pumps produce a lot of air but at a pressure too low to push the air to the bottom of a deep aquarium. Others might produce a lesser quantity but at a higher pressure. Always speak to a knowledgeable aquarium store employee about the right-size pump for your needs. Vibrator air pumps use very little electricity, and repair kits that include spare diaphragms are available for most models.

Filtration Processes

There are three major and distinctly different types of filtration: mechanical filtration, biological filtration, and chemical filtration. Many filters perform more than one of these processes.

Mechanical filtration: Simply put, mechanical filtration is the trapping of suspended particulate matter in the water by passing it through a filtering medium. This helps maintain your aquarium's water clarity. With time, the filter medium will clog and impede water flow and must be replaced.

Biological filtration: The breakdown of fish wastes and uneaten bits of food present in the aquarium produce organic compounds that are highly toxic to fish. Primary among these is ammonia. In the two-step process of biological filtration different types of bacteria first break down the ammonia into the slightly less toxic nitrates, and then to minimally toxic nitrates. This process is known as *nitrification*. The nitrates produced are usually removed from the aquarium by performing regular partial water changes (see Aquarium Maintenance). These beneficial bacteria can grow on any substrate

Hint: Ammonia is much more toxic to fish when the water is alkaline. Under acidic conditions ammonia is in the form of the much less toxic ammonium ion. If your water source is on the alkaline side, take particular care in monitoring ammonia levels until the biological activity of your filter becomes well established.

in the aquarium. In a biological filter we maximize this effect by providing a volume of some inert material with a large surface area that these bacteria can colonize.

Important note: In a new aquarium it takes some time for the beneficial nitrifying bacteria to become established. After adding your first few fish the ammonia level will over a few days rise to harmful levels. Gradually, as the ammonia-digesting bacteria become established it will fall, but the nitrite levels will then rise. After several more days the number of bacteria that feed on nitrites increases to the point where the nitrite level falls to zero. There are many brands of water-testing kits and meters available that test for these nitrogenous compounds. It is imperative that this be done on a daily basis for newly set-up aquariums until the nitrite levels have become undetectable. After this is accomplished, testing should be done on a weekly basis, or more frequently after you have added additional fish.

Chemical filtration: In chemical filtration a chemically active substance is used to remove pollutants from the water. Depending upon the medium used, these pollutants can be nitrogenous or chemical in nature. Chemical pollutants include heavy metals, the minerals responsible for water hardness, and medications. The most

A small box filter filled with carbon is an excellent way to remove unwanted medications from your aquarium. A top layer of filter floss can be used to prevent the carbon from becoming clogged with debris.

commonly used chemical filtration medium is activated carbon. With time, all chemical-filtration media lose their effectiveness and must be replaced.

Selecting Your Filter

There are two basic types of aquarium filters, air-driven and motor-driven. In general, air-driven filters are most suited for smaller aquariums, whereas one of the motor-driven models is the best choice for large tanks. Adult piranhas require large aquariums, and it is imperative that you select a filter adequate for its gallonage.

Air-Driven Filters

Inside box filters: These air-driven filters are basically small plastic boxes that house the filter media and are fitted with a perforated and removable lid. During operation, water enters through the perforated top and after passing through the filtering media is returned to the aquarium. Depending on what filter media you use these filters can perform all three types of filtration. Box filters are best suited for aquariums smaller in size than those used to house all but very small piranhas, but when filled with activated carbon are excellent for removing medication from the water after treatment is complete.

Sponge filters: Of simple construction and very low cost, sponge filters provide surprisingly good biological filtration and moderate mechanical filtration. They are available in many differ-

Sponge filters of appropriate size are an excellent choice for a small quarantine or hospital tank.

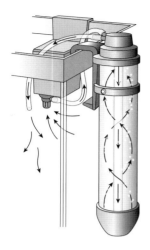
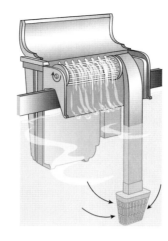

The fluidized bed filter (left) provides excellent biological filtration, but a bio-wheel filter (right) provides all three types of filtration.

ent sizes suitable for the smallest aquariums up to those of about 30- or 40-gallon (114–152 L) size. They are easily cleaned by squeezing them out under a stream of running water. Sponge filters are particularly recommended for quarantine and hospital aquariums less than 50 gallons (190 L) in size. Because they do not trap small fish, sponge filters are an excellent choice for aquariums housing baby fish.

Undergravel filters: These filters consist of a perforated plastic filter plate that covers the bottom of the aquarium, and one or more associated air lift tubes. A 1-to-3 inch (2.5–7.6 cm) layer of aquarium gravel must cover the filter plate. During operation water is drawn downward through the gravel and filter plate and then returned to the aquarium via the lift tubes. The gravel acts as the filter medium as well as the media that is colonized by the nitrifying bacteria. A big problem with undergravel filters is that they rather quickly become clogged with debris. This limits the water flow through them as well as taking up space that

the bacteria can colonize. It can also produce exceedingly high levels of nitrates and a severe drop in the pH of the water. There are specially constructed gravel washers available to help clean the gravel of this debris, but they are messy to use and require that you place your hands in the tank with your piranhas.

Nowadays I discourage the use of undergravel filters. Although they are inexpensive and at one time were considered the best biological filters available, their time has passed. There are now several types of biological filters being sold that not only do a better job, but are more easily serviced and cleaned. Two of the best are the bio-wheel hang-on filters and canister filters.

Motor-Driven Filters

Hang-on power filters and bio-wheel filters: These excellent filters provide all three types of filtration and come in sizes suitable for aquariums up to at least 100 gallons (380 L). For larger aquariums two or more can be used simultaneously. These filters hang from the top rim of the aquarium. A low-wattage motor moves water into the filter from the aquarium, and through the filter media before it passively returns to the aquarium via an overflow lip. The filtering media is usually some combination of a sponge, filter floss, or chemical filtration material. The filter media is easily observed to determine when it requires cleaning, and replacement is easily done.

An improvement in their design is the biological wheel filter. In this type, before the water is returned to the aquarium it first passes over a revolving, corrugated wheel. This wheel serves as a substrate for the growth of large numbers of nitrifying bacteria. This design also ensures that the water is thoroughly oxygenated before returning to the aquarium. They are highly recommended.

Canister filters: These filters are located outside of the aquarium. Their motor pulls water from the aquarium through a section of flexible tubing into the canister. In this pressurized container the water is forced through a series of different filter media before it is returned to the aquarium through another section of flexible tubing. If you select the filter media carefully, canister filters can provide exceptional biological, mechanical, and chemical filtration. There are models available that can be successfully used on aquariums as large as 200 gallons (760 L). Clogging of the media is indicated by a slow reduction of the return water flow. The disadvantages of canister filters are that they can be difficult and messy to clean, and are prone to leaks if all connections are not fully tightened.

Trickle filters: Also known as wet/dry filters, trickle filters provide exceptional biological fil-

A recent innovation is the inclusion of a trickle filter within a full canopy aquarium hood.

tration, as well as mechanical filtration. They also permit the addition of chemical filtering medium. Shortly after the water enters the filter, it passes over a mechanical pre-filter before trickling through a container of inert material, such as bioballs, with a high surface area. The water then flows into a large sump where a water pump directs it back into the aquarium through a section of flexible tubing.

This medium serves as the home for large numbers of nitrifying bacteria and is located above the water level in the sump, and except for the thin film of water passing over it, it is exposed to the air. This access to oxygen greatly increases the efficiency of the nitrifying bacteria as well as fully oxygenating the aquarium water before it is returned to the aquarium. Trickle filters can be very expensive as well as bulky. They are usually placed under the aquarium and hidden from view within a cabinetlike aquarium stand. Maintenance requires regular cleaning of the pre-filter. Trickle filters are most appropriate for very large aquariums where other types of filters would be inadequate. Some public aquariums have designed trickle filters for tanks in the thousands of gallons.

A recent innovation is the inclusion of a modified trickle filter as part of a full aquarium hood. Depending on their design and flow rate, these can be highly efficient filters that do not require any additional space.

Fluidized bed filters: This is a fairly new type of aquarium filter. It is designed to provide exceptional biological filtration but nothing else. You would still need to install a second filter for needed mechanical and chemical filtration. When in use, aquarium water is pumped upward through a chamber partly filled with an insoluble sand before it is returned to the aquarium. The sand serves as a substrate for the growth of large numbers of nitrifying bacteria. I think they are most suited to extremely large public aquarium displays or heavily stocked, large marine aquariums.

pH

pH is a measurement of the hydrogen (H+) ions and the hydroxl (OH-) ions in the water. A higher percentage of hydrogen ions makes the water more acid. Conversely, hydroxyl ions increase its alkalinity.

Many aquarists have been taught to be overly concerned with pH. Piranhas do very well within a pH range of at least 6.0–7.5. Gradual fluctuations cause no problems, but sudden changes can be very harmful. Any deliberate changes in your aquarium's pH should be done slowly. The major cause of pH instability in an established aquarium is poor husbandry techniques. A severe drop into the acidic zone is usually a result of pollution from an excessive buildup of organic matter in the aquarium and/or its filters. Because of a lack of buffering calcium salts, very soft water reacts more quickly and severely to these factors.

Obtaining Your Piranhas

Know the Law

Before you decide to set up a piranha aquarium contact your local Fish and Wildlife Department. In many states it is illegal to import or possess living piranhas, and severe penalties are a real possibility for anyone ignoring these laws. It is also a criminal offense for a tropical fish dealer to ship piranhas to any destination where they are illegal. These laws are based on the fear that released piranhas might be able to establish a breeding population. This happened once in a lake in Florida, requiring the chemical removal of all its fish. Although such a precaution might seem warranted in our most southern region, it seems a bit of an overreaction that many of our northern states, such as New York, where piranhas could never survive and reproduce, also ban them.

Selecting Healthy Piranhas

Use the same criteria in selecting your piranhas that you would use for other aquarium fish. A healthy fish is active, alert, and feeds readily. Avoid any fish that appears emaciated or sluggish, or has cloudy eyes or excessive mucus production covering the body or fins. These can all be signs of disease or poor aquarium conditions. Check carefully that they do not exhibit signs of respiratory distress, as this can indicate the presence of gill flukes, bacterial gill disease, or poor water quality.

Most imported piranhas will show mild to moderate fin damage as a result of the fin-feeding behavior of so many species. This could have occurred in nature before they were captured, or in the exporters' holding tanks. Most American pet shop owners know enough to

A healthy piranha, such as this subadult Serrasalmus compressus, *will be alert, active, and show no signs of skin lesions or cloudy eyes, but a few nipped fins is nothing to worry about.*

house their piranhas one per tank. Fins regenerate quickly; if the missing portions are not excessive and there is no sign of secondary bacterial or fungal infections, this alone should not discourage a potential purchase.

Transportation

Piranhas of all but the smallest sizes have the well-deserved reputation for biting through plastic aquarium bags, even when they are of double or triple thickness. My recommendation is to bring them home in a picnic cooler chest or a plastic bucket with a lid. If you must ship your piranhas home, a good idea is to place each fish in its own plastic snap-top container in which you have first drilled several small holes. This container, which should be large

A mandatory quarantine for all species of animals has long been a required procedure at zoological gardens and aquariums.

enough for your piranha to swim normally, is then placed inside a larger plastic fish bag filled with an appropriate amount of water. The bag is then oxygenated and tied shut in the normal manner with a rubber band. Doing this prevents the piranha from biting through the bag but gives them the benefits of the large amount of water it contains.

Quarantine

It cannot be emphasized too strongly that all newly obtained piranhas—and all other aquarium fish, for that matter—should undergo a quarantine period before being added to your display aquarium. This not only helps prevent the introduction of potential pathogens, but also gives the new fish time to settle down and become adjusted to aquarium conditions and diet. If more hobbyists took the time to quarantine all new fish, the incidence of diseases, parasitic infections, and unexplained deaths would be greatly minimized.

A quarantine aquarium should be set up in a simple manner for ease of cleaning and sterilization between periods of use.

The quarantine aquarium need not be anything fancy. It must only be large enough to comfortably house the fish being treated and equipped with a fully activated filter (one or two sponge filters are a good choice). Tank furnishings should also include a thermostatically controlled heater, thermometer, and possibly one or two smooth rocks or pieces of bogwood to provide security and a hiding place. A light is not required, but a glass cover is recommended to prevent the fish from jumping out and to help keep the water temperature stable. Such a simple setup permits ease of cleaning and sterilization after use.

The quarantine period should be a minimum of three weeks if no problems arise, but can be lengthened if conditions warrant. During quarantine the fish should be carefully examined at least twice daily, and at the first signs of any illness appropriate treatment should be initiated. It might take a few days for your piranha to start accepting the foods that you offer, so be diligent about promptly removing any uneaten food. In my opinion it is wise to treat all new fish, whether wild caught or captive raised, for external gill and body flukes.

Acclimatization

It is important that you gradually acclimate your newly purchased piranha to the water conditions of your quarantine aquarium, as chances are that they differ from those at the aquarium shop. One time-tested method is to float the fish bag in your aquarium until the temperatures equalize. Then gradually, over a period of about an hour, repeatedly add a little of the tank's water to the bag. This will ensure that your fish can slowly adjust to any differences in hardness and pH between the store's water and that of your aquarium.

Another excellent method is to place your piranha plus the water in its bag into a 2- to 5-gallon (7.6–19 L.) plastic bucket. The size of the bucket should be large enough so that the water in the bag does not fill it more than 25 percent. Then using a length of airline tubing slowly siphon water from the aquarium into the bucket. A clamp can be used to slow the flow of water through the tubing. Regularly check to make certain that the bucket is not overflowing. When the bucket is just about full, the acclimatization is complete.

When the quarantine period is over, it is time to place your piranha in its permanent home. Before moving it make certain that the water in your display aquarium is of the same temperature and pH as that in the quarantine tank. If they differ by much, you will have to repeat the acclimatization steps. To keep your piranhas from biting large holes in a net you can use a large widemouthed jar to catch and transfer them from tank to tank.

Although my recommendation is to keep piranhas one per aquarium, there are many hobbyists with large aquariums who have had more or less success in keeping a few of the species in groups. Primary among these are the three species in the genus *Pygocentrus*, and *Serrasalmus geryi*. If your new specimen is being added to an established group of other piranhas, make certain that it is of the same species and size. Piranhas have an excellent feeding response and are attracted to fish that appear disoriented or frightened. Many species of piranhas, including some that in nature travel in shoals, are also known to have a well-developed sense of territoriality and will attack strange individuals. This aggressiveness is enhanced by hunger, so before adding a new fish to an established group it is recommended that you feed the group well and then turn off the aquarium's light. Both these precautions will help avoid the new comer being

Piranhas of the genus **Pygocentrus**, *such as these beautiful* **P. piraya**, *are among the best candidates for keeping in groups. But expect unprovoked aggression at any time.*

met with snapping jaws. The first few hours after the introduction are the most critical. During this period of time carefully watch your aquarium to make sure that the new fish is accepted. If there are signs of aggression, you must quickly remove the newcomer or risk having it killed. Even if all goes well it is wise to check the aquarium several times daily for the next few weeks, as sometimes the aggression develops slowly. A few nipped fins is nothing to worry about, but if you notice severe bites out of its fins and flesh and that it constantly stays hidden and doesn't even come out to feed, it is then mandatory to remove it to a separate aquarium.

Although piranhas will do well in a bare or minimally furnished aquarium of adequate size and filtration, they look more attractive in an aesthetically pleasing setup, and usually show fewer signs of nervousness.

1. The first step in setting up an aquarium is placing it and its stand in their permanent location. Because of their weight, moving aquariums after they are set up is extremely difficult and often results in the development of cracks and leaks. Once this is done make certain that the tank and its stand are perfectly level. To achieve this it may be necessary to place shims under the stand. An improperly leveled aquarium develops strains that can eventually cause it to split along one of its seams.

2. If you will be using gravel, make certain it is fully washed before adding it to the aquarium. If you do not intend to use living plants, only a thin layer will be required, mainly for aesthetics. Live plants will require from 1 to 2 inches (2.5–5 cm) of gravel for their roots. There are many different types, sizes, and colors of gravel available at tropical fish stores. In general the choice is yours, but to prevent uneaten food from falling out of reach between the gravel its particle size should not be more than $1/4$ inch (6.2 mm) in diameter. You should also avoid limestone and coral gravels, as they will raise the pH to levels unsuitable for piranhas.

3. Place any rocks and bogwood in a way that creates an aesthetic appearance. Make certain that they are a type that is safe to use in an aquarium. Avoid limestone and soft rocks such as the sandstones. Soft rocks that can easily be scratched with a knife often contain harmful, soluble chemicals.

Note: Be certain that all rocks are placed so they rest securely on the aquarium's bottom. If simply placed on top of the gravel they may tip over, cracking the glass or trapping fish beneath them. Many types of bogwood that are not fully saturated with water have a tendency to float. This can be mitigated by submerging it in a pail of water until it is fully saturated. A rock or brick should be used to keep it under water during this process. This can take from a couple of weeks to a few months. If you do not have this kind of time, you can attach the bottom of the wood to a suitably heavy piece of slate using screws or a piece of stainless steel wire.

4. Fill the aquarium approximately two thirds with water of the proper temperature.

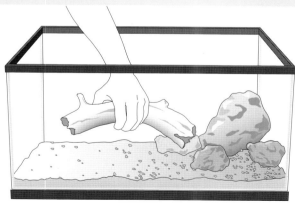

Add your thoroughly washed gravel and any rocks and bogwood.

5. Any plants, whether living or plastic, can now be planted. To create a pleasing appearance taller plants are usually placed toward the rear, with small plants in the foreground. When planting live rooted plants, first create a shallow depression in the gravel. Spread out the roots in this depression and then cover them with additional gravel. Plants that grow from a crown should have their crown level with the gravel's surface, and stemmed plants should have any leaves removed that would be buried during planting.

6. Complete the filling of your aquarium, being careful not to add the water so rapidly that it uproots the plants, and add the chlorine/chloramine neutralizing chemicals. Now is the time to install your filter, heater, and thermometer.

Note: Most municipal water districts add either chlorine or chloramine to the water supply as a means of destroying any harmful organisms. These chemicals are deadly to fish but easily removed with numerous products available at tropical fish stores. Some also precipitate any heavy metals that may be present.

7. Place the cover and aquarium light on the tank and then plug in all electrical equipment.

Note: If you have another healthy, well-established aquarium, you may wish to add a handful of gravel or filtering material from it to your newly completed setup. This will "seed" the new aquarium with beneficial nitrifying bacteria and speed the establishment of biological filtration.

Adding fish: Fish should not be added immediately. The aquarium should be watched for several days to make certain that all equipment is functioning properly. It is mandatory

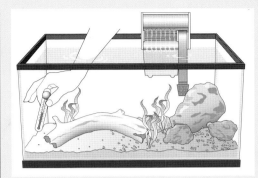

Completely fill the aquarium and add all mechanical equipment.

that when you start adding fish you do it slowly and not all at once. If the biological filtration is not fully established there is a chance of the ammonia and nitrites quickly reaching harmful levels, and it is essential that you test for them on a daily basis until the filter is fully matured. If either should rise to unacceptable levels, large frequent partial water changes can temporarily alleviate the problem until the filter matures.

To avoid the potential of your piranhas being harmed by high levels of ammonia and nitrites some people recommend that the first fish added to the aquarium not be your valuable piranhas but some hardy species, such as goldfish, to supply the nitrogenous wastes needed to establish the biological filtration. This is a good idea if you first quarantine the goldfish for a standard period of time. It would be foolish to place healthy piranhas into a tank that was possibly contaminated by sick goldfish. It is also a good idea to check your aquarium's pH once weekly, since over time it has a tendency to drop, sometimes to dangerous levels.

PIRANHA CARE AND BREEDING

Despite their ferocious reputation, piranhas are very shy fish. Newly acquired piranhas will commonly race for cover at one's approach, and show a reluctance to emerge even when fed, until the viewer has departed.

Keeping Piranhas Together

The idea of having a large aquarium devoted to either a school of one species of piranha or a group of several species is very tantalizing but most often doomed to failure. With the exception of the genus *Pygocentrus*, most piranhas at some stages in their lives feed heavily on the fins of other fish, including their own kind. This behavior is so ingrained in their makeup that it will continue even when they are well fed. There have been many attempts to keep together a group of one of the *Serrasalmus* piranhas that sometimes shoal in nature, but with few exceptions, fin predation as well as more serious forms of aggression soon become a problem. Even the larger *Serrasalmus* piranhas, that are mainly piscivorous as adults, are voracious fin predators when small. An excep-

Piranhas, such as this cariba, look their best in a well-planted aquarium.

tion might be *Serrasalmus geryi*; several people have kept small shoals of this beautiful species in large aquariums and have experienced little if any signs of overt aggression. Other possible exceptions are mentioned in the Species chapter. The chances of success in keeping several piranhas together are greatly diminished if the aquarium is overcrowded. Not only does overcrowding encourage territorial aggression, but it can also adversely affect water quality, making the fish more subject to stress and illness.

If you are determined to keep a small shoal of piranhas, I would recommend one of the red-bellied species in the genus *Pygocentrus*. These normally shoaling fish have a proven track record of frequently doing very well in groups of their own kind, and are often displayed that way at public aquariums. But even with these, minor skirmishes should be expected and one fish can suddenly, and for no apparent reason, be singled out for serious attack.

Serrasalmus geryi is one of the very few species in its genus that appear to tolerate being kept in groups.

Aggression frequently becomes life threatening when a pair has decided to spawn. There have been several encouraging reports from people successfully keeping two, or all three, of these species together in the same aquarium for prolonged periods of time. What I would not recommend is trying to add any *Serrasalmus* piranha to a tank housing a *Pygocentrus* species, as this almost invariably results in fin damage to the red-bellies.

Mixing Piranhas with Other Fish Species

The mixing of piranhas with other fish in a home aquarium is a subject of much controversy and interest. One of the most memorable piranha displays I have ever seen was at the Dallas Aquarium in Dallas, Texas. More than 30 large adult red-bellied piranhas shared a 3,000 gallon (11,400 L) heavily planted and skylit aquarium with large schools of cardinal tetras, marbled hatchetfish, bleeding heart tetras, and glowlight tetras. There were also a couple of foot-long *Pterygoplichthys* sp. catfish present for algae control. The brightly colored tetras were totally ignored by the piranhas and sparkled in the sunlight as they swam without fear among them. In addition to providing a biotope approach to displaying piranhas, it invariably amazed visitors with its beauty. In my opinion the reason for its success was quite simple: Adult red-bellied piranhas are not adapted or behaviorally programmed to feed on very small prey items. With care, it might be possible to duplicate this display at home on a smaller scale. To be successful a very large aquarium would be needed, and the piranhas would have to be large in size and the other fish considerably smaller. But since even in nature very large piranhas are known to feed on fish as small as *Astyanax* spp. tetras, success cannot be guaranteed.

One could also attempt to keep a single specimen of the large *Serrasalmus* piranhas, such as *S. rhombeus* or *manueli*, as the basis of developing a mixed-species exhibit. I have successfully maintained for several months an adult *S. sanchezi* with a few immature *Pyrrhulina* sp. characins and a pair of the dwarf cichlid *Apistogramma bitaeniata* in a heavily planted aquarium of only 50 gallons (190 L) size. The cichlids even spawned and raised a group of young.

A totally different approach can be used when attempting to add other fish to an aquarium housing *Pygocentrus* species. In nature, subadult red-bellied pacu (*Piaractus brachypomus*) are mimics of the red-bellied piranha, and have been observed shoaling with them. There have been several reports of these species coexisting peaceably in an aquarium. When I was employed at the Dallas Aquarium, we experimentally placed two 12-inch pacus in a 500-gallon (1,900 L) reserve tank containing nine adult *P. nattereri*. This group lived amiably together for a number of months until the piranhas were transferred for display purposes. (The pacus were not used because we didn't want this highly herbivorous species to consume the aquatic plants in the display aquarium.) If you wish to try mixing pacus with your piranhas, make certain beforehand that you

Hint: If you feel that you must offer live feeder fish to your piranhas, they should first receive a standard quarantine of at least three weeks' duration that includes a treatment with Praziquantel for flukes. This requires the inconvenience of permanently devoting a quarantine aquarium to feeder fish. Living foods that pose less of a threat to your fish are earthworms and adult brine shrimp. Both are eagerly consumed by most piranhas of appropriate size.

know of someone who will be willing to take your pacus after they outgrow your aquarium; *never* release them or any exotic species of fish into local waterways. There have been far too many "piranha" scares in the media after a pacu that someone had released was caught by a fisherman and identified as a killer piranha.

Feeding Your Piranhas

In nature, piranhas consume a varied diet that can differ considerably among species. Fortunately for the piranha hobbyist, most species are very adaptable and do not require you to provide them with exactly the same foods that they might eat in nature. As an example, you do not have to go so far as to provide fin-feeding species with large numbers of live fish from which they can crop pieces of fins whenever they are hungry. Whole small fish can be a satisfactory and well-accepted substitute. But you should offer some vegetable matter in the form of fruit, vegetables, and beans to piranhas known to be highly omnivorous, such as those in the genus *Pristobrycon*. In caring for the seed-eating five-cusped piranha, adding small

tion might be made for a newly captured fish that is so shy and reluctant to consume dead foods that it is losing weight. In this case, getting it to feed, even if it means tempting it with a live fish or two, is better than watching it starve.

seeds to its diet can be the difference between success and failure in keeping it healthy.

Potential Danger of Live Foods

There is a certain small segment of the aquarium hobbyists that seems to delight in watching their piranhas mutilate and devour other live fish, even though live feeder fish are not required to keep them healthy. More important, this practice poses significant threats to the well-being of your fish. Feeder goldfish and minnows are notorious for the plethora of internal and external parasites and diseases that they may carry and transmit to your piranhas. Ick, flukes, anchor worms, hexamita, and mycobacteria are just a few of the potentially serious problems that can be introduced into your aquarium with live feeder fish.

Newly purchased piranhas may at first appear reluctant to accept nonliving foods, but this is more an expression of their shyness. Until your piranhas become accustomed to the presence of people all that may be needed is for you to withdraw for a while after feeding your fish. In an hour or two all uneaten food should be removed. In nature, piranhas are opportunistic scavengers, their excellent sense of smell making it easy for them to locate appropriate food items. An excep-

Frozen Foods

A varied assortment of frozen foods should be the basis of your piranhas' diet. The process of freezing destroys almost all of the larger parasites and protozoa while maintaining the nutritional value. Freezing has no effect on some viral and bacterial pathogens, such as the causative agent of fish tuberculosis, but a well-balanced diet based on a variety of frozen foods helps keep your fish in optimum health and thus increases their resistance to disease.

The following are some of the best frozen foods for your piranhas:

Whole bait minnows and other small fish: These can make up the major portion of most piranhas' diets. They have the nutritional value of whole fish and provide an excellent source of many vitamins and minerals. Frozen small fish of several species are stocked by most aquarium shops and bait stores. The most common are golden shiners, fathead minnows (and their xanthic domestic form known as rosy-reds), and silversides. If you have difficulty finding them sold frozen, most bait stores and many pet shops carry live golden shiners and fatheads that you can then freeze at home. I do not recommend frozen feeder goldfish because their flesh contains thiaminase, an enzyme that breaks down the

Red-bellied piranhas are kept in groups more often than any other species, frequently in large public aquarium displays.

important B vitamin, thiamine. Frozen minnows are easily stored, convenient to use, and easily recognized by your piranhas as a food item. Thaw them at room temperature before feeding.

Frozen krill: Other excellent frozen foods are the krills, *Euphasia superba* and *E. pacifica*. Not only do these small marine shrimp relatives provide protein, but their exoskeletons are a rich source of trace elements and carotenes that help in the development and maintenance of orange and red pigments. *Euphasia superba* are about the size of a cocktail shrimp and excellent for most medium-size or adult piranhas, while the considerably smaller *E. pacifica* is best for small juvenile specimens.

Other Recommended Foods

Strips of lean meat such as trimmed beef heart, and pieces of shrimp and fish sold in supermarkets for human consumption can help vary your piranhas' diets. Many piranhas will also readily accept vegetable foods such as frozen or cooked fresh peas, lima beans, and string beans.

Most piranhas will steadfastly refuse to accept most freeze-dried and processed dry flake and pellet foods. There is a better chance of success when you are working with young fish. Even then, dry foods should be considered only as a supplement and not as a major portion of a piranha's diet.

Moving a Piranha

At times it is necessary to move a piranha into a different aquarium. Its quarantine period might be completed and it is time to move it into its permanent home, or an injured or sick specimen must be removed to a convalescent aquarium for treatment. Always use a net large enough to comfortably house the fish and never catch more than one piranha at a time. When piranhas are netted, they usually bite savagely at the net, so complete the transfer as quickly as possible to prevent it from biting through and falling to the floor. A frightened piranha flopping on the floor snaps defensively at anything that comes close, including your hand! This is why I recommend quickly transferring the netted piranha to a bucket of water siphoned from the aquarium and transferring it in this.

Breeding Piranhas at Home

For many aquarists the ultimate challenge is successfully breeding their favorite fish at home. Breeding piranhas is not easy. It requires a large aquarium, a considerable outlay of money and time, and having a true pair that is more interested in breeding than devouring each other.

In the past, most reported reproduction of captive piranhas occurred at public aquariums where a shoal of one species was being kept in a display tank of at least 1,000 gallons (3,800 L), but this is slowly changing. The increasing popularity of piranhas, together with the recent increase in the number of species available, has resulted in a growing number of successful spawnings in home aquariums. As far as I can ascertain, all aquarium spawnings have involved piranhas from the genera *Pygocentrus* or *Serrasalmus*. With few exceptions, a nest of sorts was constructed within natural or artificial plants, or some other synthetic substitute. It is not known whether all piranhas, especially those belonging to what are assumed to be the less highly evolved species in the genera of *Pygopritis*, *Pristobrycon*, and *Catoprion*, practice a similar form of reproduction. It is hoped that dedicated home aquarists will soon have

You should never hold your hand under a net that contains a piranha.

the answers to this and other questions about piranha reproduction.

With very few exceptions, piranhas are not sexually dimorphic, meaning that males and females do not differ significantly in appearance. The exceptions are noted in the next chapter under the individual species' discussions. To the practiced eye, females filled with eggs appear heavier than males, and it is known that several species of piranhas, including *Serraslmus sanchezi* and *S. gouldingi*, become very dark in color during the breeding season and may develop a beautiful iridescence on their sides with their small scales sparkling with iridescent blues and purples. In a few of these, such as the black piranha, males are thought to become darker than females, but at present this is conjecture, and the depth of color may also vary throughout a species' range. In the several spawnings of red-bellied piranhas I observed at the Dallas Aquarium, the breeding pair became slightly darker in color and their iridescent body spangling intensified.

Obtaining Your Breeders

I would strongly recommend that a novice at breeding piranhas start with the red-bellied piranha, *Pygocentrus nattereri*. It is attractive, and the most reasonably priced piranha. It is not surprising that this species has been bred in captivity more frequently than any other piranha. Being a shoaling species, there is a greater chance of a group coexisting than would be the case with one of the solitary fin feeders. But remember, there is still always the risk of occasional, unpredictable, serious aggression.

If you are serious about breeding piranhas, do not consider an aquarium smaller than 100 gallons (380 L) for a breeding pair of a medium-size species. The larger or notoriously aggressive piranhas, such as the *Serrasalmus rhombeus* or *S. manueli*, would require proportionately larger quarters. Large piranhas are infrequently imported. This is because their size and need for individual bagging makes the cost of shipping prohibitively expensive. There is also the chance of them biting through their shipping bags and arriving dead. Once they arrive at the aquarium store, most piranhas must be housed individually, taking up a lot of tank space. All of these factors contribute to the very high retail price for large piranhas of any species. It is far better, and much more economical, to buy a group of small fish and then raise them to maturity at home. Young fin-feeding *Serrasalmus* and *Pristobrycon* piranhas would have to each be raised in its own aquarium, or a partitioned larger one. If you have the room and can afford it, always buy more fish than you think you will need. This will give you a better chance of having a true pair.

Emulating Nature

Assuming that you have a true pair of piranhas, there are a few things you can do that might help put them in a reproductive mood. We have learned that in nature piranhas start to spawn at the beginning of the rainy season as rivers begin to rise. During the dry season most of the rivers and streams slow their flow and their temperatures rise. The increased warmth, lack of water movement, and decay of accumulated organic matter cause a significant drop in dissolved oxygen levels. In isolated lakes food is at first abundant and piranhas gain a lot of weight, but soon their food source is depleted

Red-bellied pacu (upper) are mimics of the red-bellied piranha, and the two species often do well together in an aquarium. These were caught in the Amazon River near Iquitos, Peru.

and they are forced to fast. With the onset of the rainy season, frequent showers cool the water, dilute the buildup of noxious chemicals, reduce the water hardness, and increase its oxygen saturation. All this has a stimulating effect on the fish. As the water continues to rise, the fish can move into areas with a greater abundance of food, and rapidly improve in condition. Soon they are ready to spawn.

> **Hint:** When attempting to breed one of the fin-eating, solitary species of piranhas, you might wish to keep the pair separated with a glass partition. This will permit them to see and court each other, but prevents outbreaks of serious aggression. The partition can be removed when the pair is showing a reproductive interest in each other.

During the low water season, river flows decrease, water temperatures rise, and dissolved oxygen levels fall. Rio Orosa, Peruvian Amazonia.

To simulate the dry season in your aquarium reduce the amount and frequency of feedings and raise the water temperature into the low to mid 80s°F (27–30°C). You can also reduce the volume and frequency of partial water changes, always being careful not to endanger the health of your fish. After a couple of months slowly reduce the water temperature to the mid or upper 70s°F (21–26°C), increase the frequency of feedings, and reinstate large and frequent partial water changes. If all goes according to plan, you might soon start to observe the beginnings of courtship.

The Breeding Aquarium

In addition to being spacious, the breeding aquarium should be provided with several hiding places in the form of large pieces of bogwood or rocks. A nesting site can either be a thickly planted portion of the aquarium or some artificial substrate such as a mat of artificial grass.

The ever more frequent capture of released tropical fish in local waters is a major cause of the increasingly restrictive state and local legislation affecting the fish hobby.

Courtship

Frequently, the first sign of courtship is a male piranha starting to pursue and display to a female. Displays may take the form of body waggling, or a pair swimming in tight head-to-tail circles. Pairing and courtship can be quite rough, but if the resulting injuries are only minor, it is probably best not to intervene too soon but let the two fish work out their differences. As the pair bond strengthens, the two fish will begin to aggressively defend a specific territory and start clearing this future nesting site of superfluous plant material, gravel, and debris. At this time it is best to remove any other piranhas that might be sharing the aquarium.

Spawning Behavior

During the act of procreation the pair will repeatedly circle within the nest. Periodically the female will be seen to tremble slightly as she deposits a batch of eggs that are immediately fertilized by the male. The complete spawning can take up to several hours. When it is completed, either both parents will guard the eggs, or only one will stay on the nest while the other protects its territory. Spawns can number up to several thousand eggs that hatch in two

Head-to-tail circling can be a sign of early courtship or just a test of dominance. This is a pair of pirayas.

to four days. The fry become free-swimming after an additional few days and are large enough to consume live newly hatched brine shrimp nauplii. You can buy cans of vacuum-packed brine shrimp eggs at most larger aquarium stores, and they are easily hatched at home by following the instructions on the container. Piranha fry are very sensitive to deteriorating water conditions, so be diligent in siphoning any uneaten food from the aquarium and doing daily partial water changes. With good care the fry will grow rapidly and soon be large enough to eat other foods. Commercially available frozen foods of suitable size, grated fish flesh, lean meat, and shrimp are all good choices.

Disposing of Unwanted Piranhas

The time to think about what you will do with unwanted piranhas is *before* you acquire or attempt to breed them. Piranha spawns are large to huge in size. Unless you own a large fish hatchery, there is no way that you can raise them all. Aquarium stores usually will not buy them until they have reached at least 1 inch (2.5 cm) in length, and there is no way that you can successfully raise 1,000 piranhas to that size in a 100-gallon (380 L) aquarium. They are also rather difficult to give away. Frequently, the only answer is to use the fry to feed your other fish or to euthanize the extra. It is better to raise 100 healthy fry rather than 500 sickly runts. Surplus adult piranhas are less of a problem because most aquarium stores will gladly buy or accept them as trade.

Whatever you do, remember to *never*, under any circumstances, release a piranha—or any other exotic fish species—into waterways where they are not native. They can introduce exotic fish diseases into the wild or become a harmful invasive species. It is also illegal, with stiff penalties for anyone who violates these regulations. And don't forget the fear factor involved when someone catches a piranha while fishing in a neighborhood pond!

Careful observation and routine maintenance, although not very time consuming, are essential for the health of your fish and beauty of their aquarium. Neglect results in deteriorating water conditions that will seriously compromise your fish's health.

Daily Care

Examine all fish for signs of injury or disease. Remove any uneaten food. Check the water temperature for any unexplained change. Make sure all aquarium appliances, such as heaters and filters, are working properly.

Hint: Many aquarists do not realize that a heater's pilot light will remain lit when the heating element breaks or burns out.

Weekly Care

Algae: Clean algae from the front glass of the aquarium as needed. Because it is never a good idea to place your hands into a piranha aquarium, I recommend using either a magnetic algae cleaning device or one that is attached to a long handle. Some piranhas will ignore a suckermouth algae-eating catfish, but others will consider it just another meal. Because of piranhas' sensitivity to many chemicals I would not recommend using a chemical algaecide without prior thorough testing.

Water Changes

Weekly partial water changes are standard procedure for all aquariums. No matter how efficient your filter is, there is still a slow buildup of harmful organic chemicals and hormones, including nitrates, in an aquarium housing fish. In general, a 15–20 percent water change weekly is recommended. This should be combined with a thorough siphoning of accumulated wastes and mulm from the substrate. A gravel-washing device is most helpful in the removal of this debris. Be certain that the water you add is the same temperature as that in the aquarium, and don't forget to use a water conditioner to eliminate chlorine and chloramine.

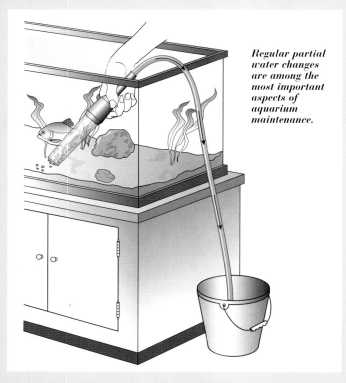

Regular partial water changes are among the most important aspects of aquarium maintenance.

MAINTENANCE

Water Tests

Established aquariums should have their water tested weekly for ammonia and nitrite levels, and for pH, but more frequently in new setups and after you have added a medication or another large fish. If you have been practicing good husbandry, ammonia and nitrite should be undetectable, but pH has a tendency to slowly drop over time. The weekly partial water change is one of the best ways to keep the pH stable.

Filters

Check weekly that the filter medium does not need cleaning or replacing. It is easy to directly observe the medium in many bio-wheel hang-on and trickle filters, but in canister filters clogging is indicated by a reduced water flow back into the aquarium. If you are using a power filter, it is a good idea to clean the motor's impeller when cleaning the medium. A buildup of slime or foreign matter on the impeller reduces the filter's efficiency and can result in a burned-out motor.

Hint: Because the nitrifying bacteria responsible for biological filtration live within the filter medium, you should never clean or replace more than 50 percent of a filter's medium at one time. If you replace all the media at once, you have in effect destroyed your aquarium's biological filtration.

Safety Precautions

Feeding and servicing your aquarium should always be performed in such a way as to mini-

Magnetic algae cleaning devices work well and eliminate the need to place your hands in the piranha aquarium.

mize the chances of a severe piranha bite. Most aquarium fish—piranhas included—quickly become conditioned to feeding times and procedures. Anticipating a meal, they rush to the surface as soon as they see a piece of food or other object enter the aquarium—even the aquarist's fingertip! These accidents usually happen the moment the fingertip enters the water, and not after the entire hand is submerged.

Piranhas are not by nature aggressive to their human caretakers. At public aquariums an aquarist may regularly enter the piranha aquarium to clean the glass or rearrange the aquascape. At these times the piranhas demonstrate their inherent shyness and suspicious nature by retreating to the far corners of the display.

HEALTH PROBLEMS AND DISEASES

One of the greatest challenges for tropical fish hobbyists is the rapid and accurate diagnosis of fish health problems and diseases.

Drug Sensitivity

Serrasalmins in general are extremely sensitive to several of the most widely used aquarium pharmaceutical drugs, making it imperative to read the ingredients listed on the label before adding any medications to a piranha aquarium. Primary among these are malachite green, and Dylox® (also known as Masoten). Malachite green is an ingredient in many of the medications sold for the treatment of ich and other diseases caused by parasitic external protozoa. If it must be used, always use it half strength. Dylox is another matter entirely; Serrasalmins are so sensitive to it that it should never be used. Frequently this drug is listed by its chemical name, 0, 0-dimethyl - 2,2,2- trichloro -1- hydroxyethyl phosphonate or 0,0- imethyl-1-hydroxy-2-trichloromethyl

This immature red-bellied piranha is suffering from a moderate case of ich.

phosphonate. To make it easier to remember, look for the 2, 2, 2- *trichloro* section.

Prevention

It cannot be stressed too strongly that an ounce of prevention is worth a pound of cure! Prevention should begin with learning as much as you can about piranhas *before* purchasing them. This, combined with careful selection of healthy-appearing specimens, followed by a mandatory quarantine period of at least three weeks, are the most important steps that a hobbyist can take to prevent outbreaks of disease. With the exception of flukes, and possibly intestinal worms, I do not recommend the prophylactic use of medication during quarantine unless the fish is demonstrating signs of illness.

Never forget that poor water quality increases a fish's susceptibility to diseases and can also cause symptoms that mimic those of

This red-bellied piranha shows the result of severe aggression by others of its species.

several serious illnesses. For instance, high ammonia levels or excessive acidity will cause an oversecretion of the fish's protective slime, giving the appearance that the piranha is suffering from an external protozoan disease. Before medicating your fish always test the water quality. Sometimes all that is required is a partial water change. Adding a medication to an aquarium where the problem is nothing more than unsuitable water conditions will only worsen the problem.

The Hospital Aquarium

An important tool for the treatment of fish, especially when the problem is not contagious, is the hospital aquarium. The setup is the same as that of a quarantine tank. When dealing with highly contagious diseases such as ich and flukes it is better to treat all the fish in their

> **Important Note:** Before adding any medication to your aquarium remove all carbon from your filters, as it removes most drugs, dyes, and antibiotics from the water.

original aquarium. The water in the hospital aquarium should closely match that of the main tank. To reduce stress, the lighting should be subdued and a hiding place provided.

Wounds

Arguably, the most common malady of captive piranhas is wounds. These can vary from very minor to life threatening and are most frequently the result of aggressive behavior by other piranhas sharing their aquarium or shipping bag. As previously mentioned, keeping several piranhas together is an invitation for trouble.

Contrary to their reputation for aggressive ferocity, piranhas are very shy and easily frightened. Injuries often occur from a badly frightened piranha crashing wildly around its aquarium. This is one of the leading causes of abrasions, split fins, and injured eyes. Public aquariums often use a fish tranquilizer before attempting to move a group of large piranhas from one display to another. When netting piranhas from an aquarium, always do it one fish at a time, for if several are confined in a net, they invariably inflict severe injuries on each other with their wildly snapping jaws.

Use of Antibiotics

These drugs should be used only for the treatment of bacterial infections. They have no effect on fungus or higher parasites, including protozoa. Follow manufacturers recommendations closely and do not overdose. Treatment should last a minimum of seven days unless you notice no improvement after 72 hours. This might indicate that the bacteria is resistant to that particular drug (it could also indicate that a bacteria is not actually the causative agent). Before adding a different antibiotic always remove the first one with a 50 percent water change followed by at least 12 hours of filtering the aquarium's water through fresh activated carbon.

Treatment of Wounds

Any wound, whether minor or severe, should be carefully watched for signs of secondary bacterial or fungal infection. A minor wound on a healthy piranha, especially if it involves the edges of the fins, usually heals uneventfully without an aquarist's intervention.

If you are keeping a group of piranhas together, you should promptly remove a moderately or severely injured specimen to a hospital aquarium. Piranhas often become cannibalistic toward an obviously compromised tankmate. The condition of a severely injured piranha should be checked several times daily to make certain that it appears to be healing normally without the beginnings of secondary infections. Adding about 1 teaspoonful of noniodized salt per gallon (3.8 L) of water is recommended both to reduce the osmotic stress on the piranhas and to discourage the growth of body fungus.

Bacterial Infections

The most common causative factor of bacterial infections in piranhas is the secondary invasion of wounds. Most common external bacterial infections of fish can be recognized by their rapid progression and red, bloody-looking base or margins. Internal bacterial infections are much more difficult to diagnose, but an infected fish frequently shows reddening of the fin bases and vent region. Many bacterial diseases of fish progress rapidly with fatal consequences. The earlier that treatment is initiated, the greater the chances of success.

A pressure sore on this black piranha's lip is from repeatedly rubbing its snout on the aquarium's glass. This is most likely the result of being kept in an aquarium that was too small and did not provide any hiding places. This lesion can easily become infected.

Bacterial fin and body rots: An early sign to look for is a reddening and erosion of the edges of the fins or a wound that progresses rapidly over a period as short as 24 hours. When this is observed, immediately test your water to ascertain if these symptoms are the result of poor water quality. If all water tests are within normal levels, it is time to add a broad-spectrum antibiotic to the water. Some of the best and safest are the nitrofurans. These synthetic drugs (not a true antibiotic) have the ability to be absorbed into the fish's body and achieve a therapeutic blood level to fight both internal and external bacterial infections. Other advantages are that they do not destroy nitrification

This newly imported black piranha is suffering from severe bacterial fin and body rots. The cause in this case was pH and ammonia burn resulting from poor water conditions during shipping.

and possess mild antifungal activity. There are many proprietary formulations available, and you should carefully follow the manufacturer's directions. I personally do not recommend using the various penicillins or erythromycin. Not only are many aquarium bacteria resistant to their action, but they severely impair or destroy biological filtration, resulting in a rapid and severe deterioration of water quality.

Tuberculosis (Mycobacteriosis): The causative agent of fish tuberculosis is the bacteria *Mycobacteria marinum*. It is a chronic and slowly progressive illness that is a much more common disease of wild and aquarium fish than most people realize. This is because most of the lesions are in the internal organs and not seen except on autopsy. Symptoms are usually vague and nonspecific in nature, and vary according to which organs are affected. Infected fish usually lose weight, are listless, and often separate themselves from the rest of the group. If the kidneys are affected, bloating and dropsy may develop. In advanced cases pimple-like, tuber-cular lesions will often form at the base of a fin or around the orbit. The only way to accurately diagnose this disease is by examining under a microscope a sample of a lesion that has first been stained with a special acid-fast dye. Fish tuberculosis can be spread by using infected fish as feeders, or by other fish picking at a lesion or eating the flesh of a tankmate that has died from the disease. Freezing does not kill *Mycobacteria*. It is also thought to be moderately contagious. The best defense against this insidious disease is to keep your fish in prime health and hope that their enhanced immune systems will ward off an infection. Any fish showing signs of tuberculosis should be immediately removed from a community aquarium and never used to feed other fish.

Although fish tuberculosis is not caused by the same pathogen that causes respiratory tuberculosis in humans, it still can be transmitted to people. These infections usually take the form of a nodular, non-healing skin rash of the hands. It is most common among people who

An advanced case of fish tuberculosis on a Copeland's tetra, Hyphessobrycon copelandi. *Note the loss of weight, fin destruction, and inflamed tubercular lesion on its throat.*

clean fish for a living, and has been given the name of *fishmonger's rash*. Modes of transmission are from handling infected fish or placing your hands in an aquarium that houses infected fish. People with a compromised immune system should wear rubber gloves when servicing their aquarium.

External Protozoan Parasites

Ich (white–spot disease): Without a doubt ich (pronounced ick) is the most common disease of aquarium fish. It is caused by the parasitic protozoa *Ichthyophthirius multifilis* (now you know why it is called ich for short!). No aquarium fish should have to die from ich, as it is easily recognized and treated. A fish with ich appears to have been sprinkled with fine grains of salt. These small white spots are usually first noticed on the fins but multiply rapidly. Contrary to popular belief, these white dots are not the parasites, but the nodules produced by the fish in an attempt to wall them off. The ich parasites are too small to be seen with the

naked eye. Only a portion of this parasite's life is spent on a fish. When the organism matures it leaves its host, drops to the bottom, and forms a cystlike structure. Within its capsule it repeatedly divides to form thousands of small cells. The cyst eventually ruptures, releasing a swarm of immature ich organisms, called *tomites*, that actively swim through the water seeking a fish. After a period of time spent crawling about on the surface of a fish they penetrate the outer layer of the skin and grow to maturity. The irritation from these parasites causes the fish to repeatedly scratch itself against objects in a futile attempt to rid itself of them. Left untreated, the white spots increase rapidly in number, affecting even the gills and eyes. Before death occurs the fins and skin may actually start to slough in patches. Ich is highly contagious.

Treatment is simple and effective. There are numerous ich medications available at all aquarium stores. Because piranhas are sensitive to malachite green, it is best to avoid any that have this drug as one of their ingredients. That being said, in my experience malachite green/formalin products such as Quick Cure® have proven safe and effective when used at half the recommended dosage. Follow the manufacturer's instructions and continue treatment for at least four days after all the white spots have disappeared. It is important to realize that only the free-swimming and crawler stages are vulnerable to treatment.

Slimy Skin Diseases (Blue Slime Diseases)

I am combining under this heading several separate, highly contagious diseases caused by external parasitic protozoa that infect the skin and gills of fish. *Childonella*, *Ichthyobodo* (formerly *Costia*), and *Trichodina* are three of them. The reason I am grouping them together is that they all produce very similar symptoms and respond to the same treatment. To accurately identify them to species requires the use of a moderately high-power microscope. Fish affected with any of these parasites soon start to produce copious amounts of mucus on the body and fins. This is an ineffective attempt by the fish to flush away the parasites. With time the gills become affected and the fish dies of suffocation.

All of these slimy skin diseases are easily treated; simply add 2 drops of formalin to each gallon (3.8 L) of water. Repeat this treatment in three days. (Formalin is the saturated solution of 37 percent by weight of formaldehyde in water.)

Caution When Using Formalin: Before adding formalin to your aquarium, clean the tank and its filters of any excess debris. Always maintain good aeration during treatment and regularly test the water quality for excessively high ammonia levels. No water changes are required after treatment

Hint: It is important to note that water with toxic levels of nitrogenous wastes, high bacterial count, or a dangerously low pH will produce symptoms similar to blue slime disease. If water tests show that any of these are the problem, all that is needed is large water change.

because this chemical slowly dissipates from the water. Formalin is classified as a potential human carcinogen, so avoid getting it on your skin or breathing its vapors.

Fungal Diseases

There are several internal and external fungal diseases that affect aquarium fish, but by far the most common and important of these is body fungus, also called *Saprolegniosis*. As the latter name indicates, the fungi of the genus *Saprolegnia* and related species are the causative agents. These are the same fungi that attack infertile fish eggs and dead fish. Body fungus can appear on the fins or body of a fish and resembles tufts of fuzzy cotton wool. *Saprolegnia* does not attack healthy tissue and is always a secondary invader of the dead and dying tissue of wounds and bacterial lesions. Once established on a living fish it spreads to healthy tissue by sinking rootlike hyphae into the fish's flesh. Fungus is unaffected by antibiotics, but it is sensitive to salt and many other pharmaceuticals. Malachite green is often recommended as an effective treatment for fungus, but it is toxic to piranhas at the dose needed to control fungus and should not be used on them. If caught early, fungus can be treated by the addition of one tablespoon of noniodized salt per gallon (3.8 L) of water. This concentration of salt will kill snails and aquarium plants. Nitrofurazone (not a true antibiotic) has mild antifungal properties and will also help prevent secondary bacterial infection of a fungal lesion. In advanced cases the antifungal drug Griseofulvin® has proved successful at a concentration of 38 mg per gallon (10 mg per liter) as a long-term bath. This prescription drug must be obtained from a veterinarian or physician and is rather expensive.

Parasitic Worms

The most important worm infections of aquarium fish are those caused by gill and body flukes, and intestinal nematodes.

Flukes: These are parasitic trematode worms. They are classified as monogenetic or digenetic, depending upon their mode of reproduction. Digenetic flukes require a series of different hosts before reaching maturity, whereas monogenetic flukes require only a single host. It is the monogenetic flukes that are of concern to aquarists. They are very common and potentially serious parasites of aquarium fish. Monogenetic flukes can be either live-bearers or egg-layers. The egg-laying dactylogyrids are mainly gill parasites, and the live-bearing gyrodactylids (*gyros* for short) prefer to inhabit the skin and fins. Both can be found on the same fish. Unfortunately for aquarists, virtually all of the freshwater parasitic monogenetic flukes are too small to be seen without the aid of a low-power microscope. In the confines of an aquarium both types reproduce exceedingly rapidly and contribute to many more fish deaths than is generally realized.

Gill flukes have been documented on wild piranhas. Symptoms may include "coughing" and spitting motions, breathing through one set

Fungus on the tail of a Sanchez piranha that had suffered fin and body damage by other piranhas. The cotton-wool appearance is clearly shown.

of gills at a time, flared gills, mucus secretions from gills, reluctance to feed, and labored respiration. A major diagnostic problem is that these symptoms can also be caused by anything that irritates the gills, from poor water quality to bacterial gill disease. Body flukes, although a very serious problem for many species of aquarium fish, seem less of a threat for piranhas. Symptoms are even more vague and include twitching and flashing, and possibly red pinpoint spots on the fins and body. The only accurate way to diagnose the presence of flukes is by gently taking a mucus smear from the gills or fins and examining it under a low-power microscope (50× is enough). The inexpensive kind that comes in a children's science set works well. This is really a very simple procedure. Catch the fish in a net and while holding it securely, gently take a mucus smear from the gills and fins. Depending on the size of the fish, a microscope slide or cover slip works well as a

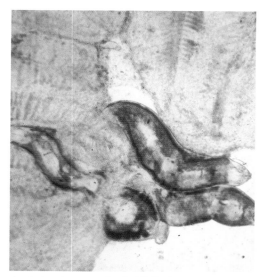

A photomicrograph of gill flukes on a wild-caught piranha. The featherlike structures in the upper half of the picture are gill filaments.

tool for this. Gently scrape the slide or cover slip in an anterior-to-posterior direction over a gill or the fish's body. When viewed under a microscope either of these types of flukes will resemble small leeches attached to the fish with hooks on the head end. They are quite active and hard to miss.

My recommendation is to assume all new fish are harboring flukes and should be treated for them while undergoing quarantine. Once they become established in your display aquarium, they can be difficult to eradicate. This is partic-ularly true of the egg-laying gill flukes because the eggs are resistant to treatment.

Just about the only effective and safe treat-ment is the drug praziquantel. It can be used as either a two-to-three-hour bath at a concen-tration of 10 ppm (parts per million) or a 24-hour-long soak at 2 ppm. Until recently this drug had to be obtained from a veterinarian, but it is now available at most aquarium stores under the trade names of Prazi-pro®, or Prazipro®. Follow directions carefully. This is a very safe drug that piranhas tolerate well.

Hint: Never use any of the common fluke remedies that include Dylox as one of their ingredients, as it is lethal to piranhas and all other serrasalmins (see Drug Sensitivity, earlier in this chapter).

Intestinal nematodes: Many wild-caught piranhas are infested with intestinal nematodes. Mild infestations are usually symptomless, but heavily infested fish may feed well but still lose weight. Sometimes a worm might actually be observed crawling out the fish's anus. Heavy worm infestations can cause severe intestinal irritation, and even intestinal perforation result-ing in fatal peritonitis. Most public aquariums deworm their fish on a yearly basis. The usual drug of choice is fenbendazole (Panacur). It can be added to the water at a concentration of 7.6 mg per gallon (2 mg per L), or added to the food at a rate of $^1/_2$ percent per pound of food. The simplest way to add this drug to a food item is to place the correct amount inside of dead feeder fish and then feed your piranha the nor-mal amount. One treatment is usually enough. This drug also kills tapeworms. Fenbendazole is a prescription drug that must be obtained from a veterinarian. It comes in both a granule and a creamy suspension, and although safe for most fish, including piranhas, it is toxic to Ictalurids (North American catfishes). There are also med-icated fish foods available to eliminate internal worms, but these are usually in the form of a dry flake or pellet not well accepted by piranhas.

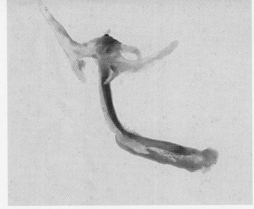

Parasitic Crustaceans

There are quite a few crustaceans that are parasites of fish, but the only ones that aquarists are likely to encounter are anchor worms and fish lice. Several species of each are widespread in nature but they are not commonly seen on imported piranhas. Almost invariably, the way they are introduced into a piranha aquarium is by the feeding of infected live feeder fish (freezing kills these parasites). The wounds that these parasites cause can easily become secondarily infected by bacteria as well as fungi.

Anchor worms are not worms at all, but copepod crustaceans of the family Lernaiidae that are highly modified for a parasitic existence. Adults resemble quarter-inch long bristles, sometimes with a forked end, attached to a fish's body or fins. The forked "tail" is a pair of egg cases. The anchor-like head is deeply imbedded in the fish's flesh and only visible when the worm is removed from the fish. Anchor worms have a complex live history involving several molts. Only the adult female is a true parasite.

Fish lice are brachiuran crustaceans belonging to the genus *Argulus*. They vary in size from one eighth to three sixteenths inch (4–12 mm) in length and somewhat resemble translucent ticks. Fish lice attach themselves to their host by means of a beak-like stylet. The toxic substances they inject into the fish plus the irritation from the stylet cause severe inflammation and local swelling.

Treatment: The treatment is identical for both of these parasites. Be forewarned that most over-the-counter remedies contain dylox, a drug that is deadly to piranhas. If only one or two of these parasites are seen on your fish you can try to carefully remove them with a pair of tweezers while holding the piranha in a net—an operation that poses a real risk of getting severely bitten

Photomicrograph of an adult anchor worm removed from a goldfish. The anchor-like head can be seen.

by the fish you are trying to help. Fortunately for aquarists the drug diflubenzuron is available. It is a safe and effective cure available to aquarists under the trade names of Dimilin® as well as Anchors Away®. It works by interfering with the crustacean's synthesis of chitin, a major component of its exoskeleton. This prevents the parasite from being able to molt. Because of this unique mode of action a cure is not immediate but may take from several days to a couple of weeks.

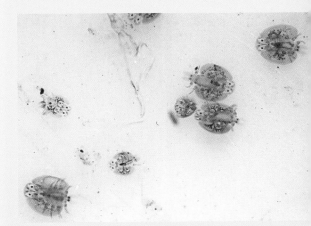

These are a few of the fish lice that had been removed from a group of feeder minnows.

More species of piranhas are being exported from South America for the aquarium trade than ever before. However, many of these specimens are misidentified or have common or scientific names applied to them that lack scientific standing. This section covers most if not all species imported with any regularity and several rare and newly described species. All measurements are total lengths (tip of snout to end of tail).

Genus *Pygocentrus*; the Red-bellied Piranhas

These three shoaling species frequently do well when kept in groups, but incidents of cannibalism can occur without warning, particularly if they are kept in overcrowded conditions or during reproduction.

Pygocentrus nattereri

Common name: Red-bellied piranha

Adult size: Approximately 12 inches (30 cm), but larger specimens are sometimes seen.

An immature Serrasalmus compressus *(above) and* Pygocentrus nattereri *caught near the mouth of the Rio Tigre, Peru.*

Range: A huge area of Amazonia, south to include the Rio Paraná and Paraguay. It is absent from the Orinoco and Guiana drainages.

Comments: This is the most familiar, commonly imported, and least expensive of all the piranhas. Many of the smaller specimens seen for sale are captive bred. In the aquarium literature it is often confused with *P. cariba* (see following species), and its range listed erroneously as including the Orinoco River of Venezuela. Red-bellied piranhas often do well when kept as a small group in a large aquarium, but incidents of aggression may occur at any time. It is the most frequently spawned of all piranha species, and the fry are easily raised.

As can be expected with a species inhabiting such a large range, there is much local varia-

This young adult red-bellied piranha was caught in the Nahuapa Channel off the Rio Tigre, Peru.

Pygocentrus ternetzi is an invalid name for this yellow form of the red-bellied piranha.

tion in color and markings among different populations. Small specimens resemble the adults but show less orange and are more heavily spotted. *Pygocentrus ternetzi* is an invalid synonym often applied to the slightly larger, yellow-bellied forms from the southern portion of its range.

Pygocentrus cariba

Common name: Cariba, black-eared piranha, *capaburro*

Size: Up to 15 inches (38 cm) and 1 1/2 pounds (670 g).

Distribution: Orinoco River and its tributaries, Venezuela, and Colombia.

Comments: This fish is the Orinoco River equivalent of the Amazonian red-bellied piranha. It appears that the habits and biology of both are similar. It is easily distinguished from its Amazon River relative by the presence of a dark humeral (shoulder) spot, a blunter face, and a slightly less deep body. Breeding adults become very dark in color, with black pigment obscuring most of the other colors and markings. This might be the source of the invalid scientific name *Serrasalmus* (or *Serrasalmo*) *niger* frequently seen in the older scientific literature and some aquarium books. This species has been bred only rarely under aquarium conditions with details of the spawning agreeing quite well with those of *P. nattereri*. At the present time tropical fish imports from Venezuela have become spo-

The cariba is the Orinoco River equivalent of the Amazonian red-bellied piranha. Its dark shoulder spot is lacking in its Amazonian relative.

The piraya is the largest of the three species in its genus and restricted to the São Francisco River system of central Brazil.

radic, resulting in less of these fish for sale and their prices escalating.

Pygocentrus piraya

Common name: Flame-sided piranha, piraya, São Francisco red-bellied piranha

Size: Up to at least 20 inches (48 cm)

Distribution: The Rio São Francisco and its tributaries, eastern Brazil

Comments: This is the largest of the red-bellied piranhas and one of the largest of any piranha. Only *S. rhombeus* and *S. manueli* have been reported to grow as big. This species and *Serrasalmus brandti* are the only piranhas known from the Rio São Francisco system. Although similar in appearance to the red-bellied piranha, all age classes show less dark pigmentation, and the rich golden yellow or orange undersides extend upward on the sides in flame-like patterns. Several hobbyists have successfully kept this fish in small groups, but this should not be taken to mean that fatal aggression is

not a very real possibility. Because of its extremely large adult size a tank of at least 150 gallons (570 L) is the minimum size that anyone should consider for maintaining this piranha, particularly if they intend to keep more than one. The piraya has not yet been spawned in captivity, but I would expect them to breed in a similar fashion to their two close relatives.

Genus *Serrasalmus*

All piranhas in this genus feed heavily on fins when young, graduating to a diet of whole small fish and fish flesh with maturity. Some also consume a considerable amount of vegetable matter. It is safest to keep these fish by themselves. They definitely should not be mixed with piranhas from other genera.

Serrasalmus manueli

Common name: Manuel's piranha

Size: Orinoco River specimens average around 15 inches (38 cm). Those from certain

Manuel's piranha is among the most massively built **Serrasalmus** *species. Rio Iriri, Brazil.*

areas of the lower Amazon have been reported to grow close to 2 feet (60 cm).

Distribution: Orinoco River basin and the Guiana Highlands of Venezuela, and the Rio Negro and other rivers of the lower Amazon drainage of Brazil. It appears to prefer clear- or blackwater habitats, avoiding whitewater regions.

Comments: This large and beautiful piranha is the most powerfully built species within its genus. It was originally described as belonging to the genus *Pygocentrus*, but this taxonomic error was soon corrected. Specimens larger than 6 inches (15 cm) are virtually impossible to confuse with any other species. They are silvery with a bluish green sheen and their operculum, throat, and pectoral fins are a contrasting rich orange red. Numerous short and narrow dark bars decorate their sides, and the tail sports a basal black V. Juveniles are more elongate, less

massively built, and have a proportionately large head and eye.

As with many blackwater fish, Manuel's piranha is reported to be quite delicate in captivity and requires water of exceptionally good quality that is low in dissolved nitrogenous wastes. A large, roomy aquarium, water of a slightly acid pH, and adequate aeration are recommended. Its delicate nature and great beauty are both responsible for its consistently high price. Definitely not a piranha for the beginner.

Serrasalmus brandtii

Common name: Brandt's piranha

Size: Based on field collections, appears to reach close to 12 inches (30 cm)

Distribution: Rio São Francisco drainage, Brazil

Comments: This species is the only *Serrasalmus* known from the Rio São Francisco drainage, a habitat it shares with *Pygocentrus*

Serrasalmus brandtii is one of only two piranhas from the São Francisco River of Brazil.

piraya. Its form is similar to many others of its genus, except that the first ray of the anal fin is positioned almost directly below the beginning of the dorsal fin instead of a bit more posterior. In color it is basically a silvery or slightly golden fish with a yellow tinted anal fin. Adults show little noticeable body spotting, and the tail shows both a dusky base and border. Young are more distinctly spotted. In nature this fish feeds mainly on the fins and flesh of other fish, with the addition of a very small amount of plant material. There have been attempts to keep Brandt's piranha in small groups, but only with limited success. Sooner or later there are episodes of aggression resulting in fin and body mutilation. There have been no reports of captive reproduction.

Serrasalmus rhombeus

Common names: Black piranha, white piranha (young specimens)

Size: One of the largest piranhas; specimens of 22 inches (56 cm) and a weight of 7 pounds are not uncommon in some areas, including the Rio Nanay of Peru.

Comments: As this species is now interpreted, it is abundant throughout the Orinoco and Amazon River systems south to Bolivia.

Discussion: This large, widespread, and variable species may be a solitary hunter or found in loosely organized shoals. Young are silvery in color with a variable number and arrangement of round, dark body spotting. In some locations a pinkish or orange wash is present on the operculum and anal fin. The iris of fish less than 4 or 5 inches (10–12 cm) is clear. The tail has a diffuse black base and terminal band. As this fish matures, it becomes progressively darker and gradually acquires the deep red eye so characteristic of this species. Some breeding adults are particularly dark in color with beautiful iridescent purple reflections. It has long been thought that *S. rhombeus* may actually be a complex of several closely related or evolving species, and recent chromosomal studies seem to bear this out.

An adult black piranha is an impressive aquarium fish and potentially very long lived. Two lived at the Shedd Aquarium for 22 and

An adult black piranha from the Rio Negro, Brazil.

An adult Goulding's piranha caught in the Rio Negro near Barcellos, Brazil.

23 years, respectively. A peculiarity of this and several other piranha species is that they appear to be relatively fast growers in nature, but this is not the case in captivity. The reasons for this are not known, but almost everyone who has kept this *S. rhombeus* has commented on how slowly they increase in size. Many piranhas of other species, particularly *S. sanchezi*, are imported and sold as black piranhas, requiring hobbyists to carefully verify their identity before purchase.

Black piranhas were bred in aquariums as early as the 1960s, when several spawns were documented at the Shedd Aquarium in Chicago. The main obstacles to successfully spawning this fish are its aggressive nature and the very large aquarium required. A few people have successfully kept this fish in small groups, but I wouldn't recommend it as a long-term policy. Younger specimens are particularly aggressive fin eaters and show no reluctance to dine on others of their own kind, and adults can suddenly and without warning become exceedingly aggressive toward conspecific tankmates—even when kept in huge quarters at public aquariums.

Serrasalmus gouldingi

Common name: Goulding's piranha

Size: Adults average 12 inches (30 cm) in length, but are considerably larger in parts of their range.

Distribution: Black- and clearwaters of the Rio Negro, and the Cassiquiare, Japurá, and Pacimoni rivers of Brazil and Venezuela. It is absent from the Amazon.

Comments: Adult Goulding's piranhas superficially resemble black piranhas, and they were confused with it until 1992, when *S. gouldingi* was described as a distinct species. Small individuals are very similar to young Manuel's piranha. Adults can be distinguished from *S. rhombeus* by their shorter snouts, amber or clear eyes, vertically elongated, dark, barlike spots on their sides, and a clear rather than black edge to their otherwise darkly pigmented tails. Breeding adults become almost black with the body spots totally obscured. At this time one should check the eye color. Virtually nothing is known about their habits in nature, but they are probably similar to other *Serrasalmus*

Sanchez's piranhas are usually found in areas of whitewater. Amazon River near Iquitos, Peru.

of similar size. My limited experience with fishing for them in Brazil seems to indicate that adults may travel in loose groups. I have not heard of any aquarium spawnings of this interesting species. Goulding's piranha is seldom imported under its own name, but one should look for it in shipments of *S. rhombeus* and *S. manueli* from Brazil.

Serrasalmus sanchezi

Common names: Diamond piranha, red-throated piranha, Sanchez's piranha

Size: Adults average $6^1/2$ to 8 inches (16.5–20 cm) in length.

Range: Abundant in the middle and upper Amazon, and lower Marañón and Ucayali rivers of Peru. Considered a whitewater species but I have caught large numbers in the Rio Orosa, a mixed black- and whitewater stream.

Comments: Young *S. sanchezi* are silvery with numerous black spots on the upper half of the body. All but very small specimens show considerable red on their throats, breasts, and anal fins. The tail has a dusky terminal band and is dark basally. Adults become darker with numerous violet and silver spangles and gradually develop reddish eyes. When in breeding condition all colors deepen, obscuring the body spots.

Sanchez's piranha is quite close in appearance to the Venezuelan *S. medinai* (see below), even though their ranges are widely separated. It has long been confused in the aquarium literature with *S. spilopleura*, and because of the adults' reddish eyes, they are frequently sold as young black piranhas. All age classes can be distinguished from most specimens of *S. spilopleura* (and its Amazonian counterpart, *S. maculatus*) by the lack of a clear edge and black subterminal band to the tail. It is more difficult to separate from immature *S. rhombeus*, but it is more laterally compressed, shows more red pigmentation, and is not quite as deep bodied. There are also differences in scale and serrae counts. It can also be confused with *S. compressus* (see below), a species that shares its range, but it lacks that fish's intense black terminal tail band, does not seem as high backed, and has round rather than vertically oval body spots.

This is a very attractive and easily maintained fin-feeding species. There are reports of it being kept in groups or with other piranha species; something I do not recommend. While I was serving as curator at the Dallas Aquarium we received more than 20 specimens of this species after they were confiscated by the United States Fish and Wildlife Service (and misidentified as black piranhas). Because we lacked room, all were placed together for several months in a 300-gallon (1,140 L) concrete trough. Only minor fin damage was observed, but the water temperature was only 72°F (22°C). When we attempted to place a couple in our 3,000-gallon (11,400 L) display of red-bellied piranhas, they quickly reverted to their fin-eating habits and had to be removed before the red-bellies became totally definned.

I have not been able to find any documented cases of this fish spawning in captivity, but with the large numbers being exported from Iquitos, Peru, and their comparatively small adult size, I would not be surprised if there have been unreported successful aquarium spawnings.

Serrasalmus medinai

Common name: Locally called *Caribito* or Palometa

Size: Approximately 6 inches (15 cm).

Distribution: Orinoco River basin, Venezuela

Serrasalmus medinai *is a common Venezuelan piranha.*

Comments: Adults of this moderately sized piranha resemble the Amazonian species *S. sanchezi.* Both have a rather robust snout, a faint humeral spot, and considerable red coloration to the operculum, throat, and anal fin. The tail markings, body spotting, and size of these two piranhas are also similar. It is frequently mentioned in the literature that young specimens resemble *P. cariba* in shape and markings. I do not fully agree with this statement, because at all ages it has the typical *Serrasalmus* feature of a concave dorsal contour to the nape region, even though it is not as greatly pronounced as in some other species.

It is surprising that this rather widespread and attractive species is not seen more frequently in shipments from Venezuela. At present there is very little information about keeping it in captivity, and I cannot find any records of it breeding in an aquarium. This is definitely a fin feeder, and I would advise anyone lucky enough to find one to keep it by itself, unless you are attempting to breed it.

Serrasalmus neveriensis
Common name: Neveri River piranha
Size: No larger than 12 inches (20 cm)
Distribution: Rio Querecual, Neveri River, Venezuela
Comments: *Serrasalmus neveriensis* was described in 1993. In the description its great similarity of form and markings to *S. medinai* was mentioned. Differences between these two fish are subtle. *S. neveriensis* is slightly more deep bodied, has a less blunt face, and has larger but fewer black spots on the body. It also shows more yellow on the throat and belly when compared with the more reddish coloration of *S. medinai.*

Serrasalmus neveriensis *appears to be a rare and local species restricted to the Neveri River system of northern Venezuela.*

This rare and local piranha has probably never been exported for the aquarium trade. I am particularly indebted to Ivan Mikolji for providing me with the accompanying photograph of a freshly collected specimen.

Serrasalmus spilopleura
Common name: Spilo, ruby-red spilo
Size: 8 inches (20 cm)
Distribution: Guaporé, Paraná, and Araguaia basins; Brazil, Bolivia, Argentina
Comments: There have been important changes in the taxonomy of this fish since the first edition of this book was published. At that time it was believed that *S. maculatus* was just a junior synonym of *S. spilopleura,* the distribution of which was thought to include the Amazon basin plus the Paraná and Paraguay rivers to the south. Now, after much in-depth research, Dr. Michael Jégu has concluded that the true *S. spilopleura* occurs only in the Rio Guaporé and

This **Serrasalmus spilopleura** *was caught in the San Martin River, Bolivia.*

possibly the upper Rio Toncantins drainages, and that *S. maculatus* is a distinct species inhabiting the rest of the range. Not all authorities agree with Jégu's conclusions, and I would not be surprised if future research once again combines them under the name of *S. spilopleura*. But for the time being I think it best to treat them as two separate but closely related species.

These piranhas are quite similar in appearance, but the Amazonian *S. maculatus* is basically a yellow fish, the true *S. spilopleura* from the Rio Guaporé is more a golden orange, and those from the Araguaia basin are red. Subadults of both *S. spilopleura* and *S. maculatus* display a distinctive black subterminal tail band margined with a clear border that may or

As with all fin-feeding piranhas, I would recommend great caution before keeping two or more of either *S. spilopleura* and *S. maculatus* together.

may not become increasingly obliterated with dark pigment as the fish matures.

The habitat of *S. spilopleura* is quite remote and fairly limited, so as can be expected, very few are being imported and they always command a higher price than the more abundant and widespread *S. maculatus*.

In spite of this fact there are several reports of aquarists having had reasonable success keeping them in groups under roomy conditions. Aquarium spawnings have also been reported. What is unclear is whether these reports involved the true *S. spilopleura*, *S. maculatus*, or both.

Serrasalmus maculatus
Common name: Yellow spilo
Size: Approximately 8 inches (20 cm)
Distribution: Widespread and abundant throughout the Amazon basin and the Pantanal region of southern Brazil
Comments: Most yellow spilos have a broad subterminal black band and a clear terminal edge to the tail, but this hyaline edge is not always present. The yellow Amazonian form of

Serrasalmus maculatus *is a widespread species throughout the Amazon Basin. Note the clear tail edge. Rio Purus, Brazil.*

Serrasalmus irritans is rather elongated and pointy snouted with numerous small body spots.

this fish can be confused with an unidentified species occasionally exported from Peru, but that piranha has reddish rather than clear eyes, a black terminal tail band, and a different pattern of body spotting.

This piranha combines the desirable traits of hardiness, moderate size, and great beauty. It is usually more moderately priced than many other species and is highly recommended to novice piranha hobbyists. See the previous discussion of *S. spilopleura* for additional information. At least one respected ichthyologist is of the opinion that the proper name for *S. maculatus* should be *S. nigricans*.

Serrasalmus irritans

Common name: None

Size: A moderately small species, with adults averaging about 6 inches (15 cm)

Distribution: Orinoco River basin, Venezuela

Comments: This is a moderately elongated and pointy snouted piranha. The upper half of its silvery body is marked with numerous dark spots that are smaller in size than those of most other piranhas, and the tail has a prominent black base that extends into the tail lobes to form a conspicuous dark V. Its anal fin and posterior portion of the head can be either pinkish red or yellow. This variation in color is range dependent. The diet of smaller specimens is made up mainly of fish fins, with fish flesh and entire small fish becoming more important as they mature. *Serrrasalmus irritans* has been observed in nature to employ the hunting techniques of both stalking its prey and sudden ambush. Because of its documented fin-feeding habits I recommend keeping this fish as a solitary aquarium specimen. This is despite the fact

Serrasalmus marginatus is a locally abundant species but infrequently imported.

that a few aquarists have been reasonably successful keeping it in small groups for varying lengths of time. There are no records of this fish spawning successfully in an aquarium.

Serrasalmus marginatus

Common name: None

Size: About 9^1/$_2$ inches (24 cm)

Distribution: Paraná and Paraguay river basins; Argentina, Paraguay, and Uruguay

Comments: In parts of its range this piranha is reported to be very abundant. As with most tropical fish from this part of South America, it is not frequently imported for the aquarium hobby. *Serrasalmus marginatus* is a moderately elongated piranha that lacks bright colors. The body is basically silver, darker on the back, with numerous black spots of moderate size. The tail, anal, and adipose fins are golden yellow, and the tail is basally black. This dark area usually covers more than half of the fin. Fish in breeding condition are said to darken considerably in color.

In nature, its diet comprises mainly fish fins and flesh, with chunks of flesh being more important to adult fish. It has also been observed picking parasitic crustaceans from the fins and skin of *Pygocentrus nattereri*. This piranha prefers areas with little current and establishes feeding territories that it aggressively defends. Its usual hunting method involves a slow stalk followed by a quick dash. I would recommend keeping this aggressive hunter as a solitary aquarium specimen.

Serrasalmus compressus

Common name: None

Size: Adults average 8 to 9 inches (20–23 cm) in length.

Distribution: Middle and upper Amazon River basin; Brazil, Peru, and Bolivia

Comments: *Serrasalmus compressus* begins our discussion of five species of notably deep-bodied and laterally compressed piranhas with vertically elongated belly serrae (*S. compressus, altuvei, geryi, altispinus,* and *hastatus*). Originally described from Brazil's Rio Madiera, it is now known to be much more widespread. I have found it, or a very similar fish, to be quite abundant in the Peruvian Amazon, where I have caught it in the whitewater Amazon main channel as well as the blackwater Rio Nanay. Piranha shipments from Peru often list this fish as either *S. sanchezi* or *S. rhombeus,* from which it can be told apart by its more pointed head, a blacker terminal tail band, and slightly oval rather than round body spotting that extends well below the lateral line. It can also be mistaken for *S. altuvei* (see next entry), a fish from Venezuela, but that fish is even higher backed, has a more slender and pointed snout, and has body markings more vertically elon-

The black spots on the body of **Serrasalmus compressus** *are oval rather than round. This piranha becomes increasingly high-backed with age. Amazon River, Iquitos, Peru.*

gated and not extending as far ventrally. Breeding adult *S. compressus* can become quite dark in color, and adults of some forms develop red eyes. This is another of the fin-eating species, and is best kept as a solitary specimen. I have not heard of any aquarium reproduction of this piranha.

Serrasalmus altuvei

Common name: Caribe azul (blue piranha)
Size: Averaging about 7–8 inches (18–20 cm)
Distribution: Clearwater tributaries of the Orinoco River, Venezuela
Comments: Adults of this species are very deep bodied and of a bluish-gray color with vertically elongated and rather faint body spotting. The dorsal profile of the supraorbital (above the eyes) region is distinctly concave. Young are more silvery and difficult to separate from young *S. compressus*, a species that does not occur in Venezuela. This piranha seems to be quite uncommon in nature. It is seldom imported and is even more rarely imported under its proper name. Usually it is labeled simply as a white piranha (the silvery young) or mistakenly as *S. rhombeus*. It is probably a fin-feeder in nature, and it is recommended that it be kept as a solitary aquarium specimen. It has not yet been bred in captivity.

This adult **Serrasalmus altuvei** *clearly shows the highly arched back typical of this Venezuelan piranha.*

Serrasalmus geryi

Common name: Black stripe piranha, Géry's piranha
Size: At least 10 inches (25 cm)
Distribution: Lower Toncantins and Araguaia rivers, Brazil
Comments: Géry's piranha is a uniquely beautiful and unmistakable species. Its almost unmarked lavender-blue body coloration combined with the broad, black predorsal stripe extending from the dorsal fin to the lower lip

Géry's piranha is one of the most distinctive and beautiful of all the piranhas.

is found in no other known species of piranha. Observations in nature appear to indicate that Géry's piranha may travel in small groups of similar-size individuals. This may explain why it has frequently shown little conspecific aggression when several are kept together in an aquarium. I would still recommend constant vigilance if you wish to try this. Géry's piranha has proved to be quite hardy but has been bred only rarely under aquarium conditions. This fish is in high demand within the hobby, and accordingly, is priced rather high.

Serrasalmus altispinus
Common name: None
Size: Not accurately known but certainly at least 10 inches (25 cm)

Distribution: Described from Rio Uatamá drainage, Brazil

Comments: Described in 2000, this fish is still not well known. In appearance it is quite similar to *S. rhombeus* but deeper bodied and with longer, more vertically oriented belly serrae. It also lacks that fish's distinctive red eye. The Rio Uatamá is a north bank tributary of the Amazon downstream from Manaus, Brazil, so I would look for this fish in shipments of black piranhas from that large city. The accompanying photograph should help in separating it from the more common *S. rhombeus*. Almost nothing is known of its biology in nature or aquarium care, but I would recommend keeping it by itself and caring for it in a similar fashion to *S. rhombeus*.

Serrasalmus altispinus is a poorly understood species described in 2000.

Serrasalmus hastatus

Common name: None

Size: The limited collection data indicate a mature size of approximately 8 inches (20 cm).

Distribution: Lower Rio Negro and its tributary the Rio Branco, Brazil

Comments: Described as recently as 2001, *S. hastatus* is another of the deep-bodied and laterally compressed piranhas. It is somewhat similar to both *S. altuvei* and *S. compressus*, but differs from both in its nearly straight dorsal head profile and a variable number of

Serrasalmus hastatus is recently described and rarely imported. Its dorsal contour is less arched than in the other high-backed species.

The elongate piranha is well named. No other species is so slender.

vertically elongated spots and thin stripes that are most numerous on the upper portion of the body. These markings are more prominent in preserved specimens. The name *hastatus* means "spear-shaped" and refers to the shape of its head. This is an infrequently collected species and considered uncommon in nature.

There is virtually no information on the aquarium husbandry of this species, but I would recommend keeping it as a solitary specimen in relatively soft and acidic water that is similar to the conditions found in the blackwater Rio Negro. I have included this species to alert readers to look for it (and the equally rare and newly described *S. altispinus*) in piranha shipments from Manaus, Brazil.

Serrasalmus elongatus

Common name: Elongate, or slender piranha

Size: Adults average about 8 inches (20 cm), but have been reported to achieve lengths close to a foot (30 cm).

Range: Amazon and Orinoco river basins

Comments: This widespread species is the most slender of the piranhas. Most often it is plain silvery-gray in color, but specimens from Venezuela often show considerable red pigmentation on the operculum, throat, and irises of the eyes. The tail has a diffusely dark basal area that is usually more pronounced on the lower lobe. The elongate piranha is a fast-swimming, solitary ambush predator that feeds heavily on the fins, scales, and flesh of other fish. In the Peruvian part of its range where it is quite common I have found it in swifter water more often than other species of piranhas. It seems to particularly like the vicinity of stream mouths, where it can wait to ambush unsuspecting prey being washed downstream. It is strongly recommended that this aggressive hunter be kept by itself, as it will readily attack any other fish, including others of its own kind. *Serrasalmus pingke* is a commonly used but invalid synonym for the Venezuelan forms.

This piranha is typical of the fish being imported under the name of **Serrasalmus gibbus.**

Serrasalmus gibbus

Common name: Castelnau's piranha has been suggested, honoring the describer Iranus Castelnau.

Size: Because of its apparent rarity, its size is not well understood.

Distribution: As far as is known, the Rio Toncantins basin, Brazil

Comments: *Serrasalmus gibbus* was described in 1855 by Castelnau, and like so many scientific descriptions from that era it is incomplete and based on only one specimen. Piranhas are sometimes seen in the pet trade that are midway in shape between *S. elongatus* and *S. rhombeus*, with a coloration that is close to the latter species. These fish agree in appearance with the drawing that accompanied the original description of *S. gibbus*, including the flat dorsal profile of the back anterior to the dorsal fin, but there is no way of determining if it is the same species or just an elongate mor-

photype of *Serrasalmus rhombeus*, the black piranha. The accompanying photograph shows a typical specimen. Note the red eyes, a trait adult specimens share with *S. rhombeus*. Because of its rarity in imports, not much has been written about its aquarium husbandry, nor has it been bred in captivity. Until this fish becomes better known I would recommend caring for it in a manner similar to *S. rhombeus*.

Serrasalmus nalseni

Common names: *Caribe pintado* (spotted piranha), Nalsen's piranha

Size: Averages 7 to 8 inches (18–20 cm) with a few slightly larger

Distribution: Known only from the Rio Uracoa and associated lakes and palm-bordered swamps (*morichales*), Venezuela

Comments: This species was poorly described by Fernandez-Yepez in 1969 from two specimens, and not recollected again until July 2007

Nalsen's piranha is a very rare and local species. Palm swamp adjoining Rio Uracoa, Venezuela. This might be the first published color photograph of the species.

when the tireless Venezuelan fish collector Ivan Mikolji revisited the Rio Uracoa and Uracoa *morichales*. After catching several specimens of this piranha, and also filming it under water, he kindly sent me the excellent photograph used in this book. This rediscovery of Nalsen's piranha was one of the most unexpected and exciting things to happen in the field of piranha biology in a long time. *Serrasalmus nalseni* can be distinguished from all similar piranhas by the extent and size of its body spots. Many of these are larger than the pupil of the eye and extend far down the sides, almost reaching the belly. Unlike the vaguely similar *S. rhombeus*, the tail of *S. nalseni* has a black base but lacks a dusky outer margin. Obviously, there is no information available on the aquarium care of this piranha, but now that it has been recollected, we can hope this will soon change.

Serrasalmus eigenmanni, serrulatus, humeralis, hollandi, and *scapularis*

This group of several very similar species is confusing to biologists and hobbyists alike. Their taxonomic validity, their relationships within the piranha evolutionary tree, and the extent of their individual ranges are still unclear. I am not calling them a complex of species because this would infer close relationships within the group, and this is probably not the case. A workable key to separate them by external appearance has not been created. It is thought by some that *S. humeralis* might actually be a synonym of *S. eigenmanni*, as *S. gymnogenys* is considered to be. Further complicating this situation is that some of these fish have at one time or other been included in the genus *Pristobrycon*. Preliminary studies using molecular biology seem to indicate that *S. serrulatus* and *S. eigenmanni* are not as closely related as their very similar appearances seem to indicate. *Serrasalmus serrulatus* might actually be most closely related to *Pristobrycon calmoni*, and *S. eigenmanni* to *S. spilopleura*. However, until the ranges of all these species become clearly understood there is the possibility that fish used in these studies were misidentified. For example, the *S. eigenmanni* specimens used in at least one of them came from Brazil and Venezuela, but the true *S. eigenmanni* might be found only in the rivers of Guiana, where it was originally described. Furthermore, what we are now calling *S. eigenmanni* and *S. serrulatus* might actually turn out to each be a complex of two or more undescribed species. I have included several photographs of fish resembling our present perceptions of these species. Most are field photos with collection data.

This fish, caught in the Rio Negro, is in many ways similar to Serrasalmus eigenmanni, *but it may well be an undescribed species.*

This fish from Peru's Rio Nanay is probably the true Serrasalmus serrulatus.

Piranha imports from South America commonly include fish listed under any of these names. They are also sometimes imported as *Pristobrycon calmoni*, a distinct species of similar shape easily separated from similar species by its black terminal tail band (see below). Hobbyists should be warned not to take these pet store appellations too seriously, but to carefully compare the fish with scientific descriptions, known ranges, and photographs of type specimens. But be forewarned that much of the literature concerning these species is frequently contradictory. Some of this information is available on the internet (see Useful Addresses and Literature). At the present time, *S. serrulatus* is the only one of these fish whose range is thought to include the upper Amazon region of Peru, so a fish labeled as *S. eigenmanni* in a shipment from Peru should be suspect. Similarly, a black marginal tail band would rule out either of these two species.

Holland's piranha, *Serrasalmus hollandi*, was described in 1874 from a single specimen caught in the Rio Guapore of southern Brazil. As described, it seems to be quite similar to *S. eigenmanni*, but a bit less deep bodied. Piranhas labeled as *S. hollandi* are occasionally being seen on dealers' lists and in the tanks of tropical fish stores. To the best of my knowledge these are all incorrectly labeled and *S. hollandi*, if it is a valid species, is not being exported. Almost all fish labeled as this species have a black terminal tail band, something lacking in the true *S. hollandi*.

The situation with *S. humeralis* and *S. scapularis* is even more confused. Jégu suggested that *S. humeralis* might be a synonym of *S. eigenmanni*. Géry placed *Serrasalmus scapularis* in the genus *Pristobrycon*, and then suggested that it might be the same fish as *S. serrulatus*. Determining the true placement of *S. scapularis* will be difficult since it was described more than 100 years ago from only one specimen. However, the drawing of *S.*

An example of one of the very puzzling and possibly undescribed species that resembles the S. eigenmanni/serrulatus *complex of species. Rio Apayacu, Peru.*

humeralis in the original description shows a fish with much smaller and more numerous spots than those described for *S. eigenmanni*.

This fish of undetermined species caught in the Rio Vermelho near Aruana, Brazil is in some ways similar to the poorly described Serrasalmus scapularis.

Until there is much more research done on this entire group I think it best to avoid any speculation about their validity and relationships.

Genus *Pristobrycon*

Because of the taxonomic uncertainty surrounding this genus several of them may be sold as either a *Pristobrycon* or a *Serrasalmus* (see genus *Pristobrycon* for more information).

Pristobrycon calmoni

Common names: Calmon's piranha, dusky palometa

Size: Approximately 6 inches (15 cm)

Distribution: Orinoco River, Venezuela, and possibly the Brazilian Amazon and Toncantins

Comments: This very deep-bodied and laterally compressed fish is the type species for the genus. There may or may not be a pattern of small faint spots on the sides and a reddish wash to the anal fin and operculum. Most specimens have only a very faint black area at the base of their tails, and its most distinctive marking is a broad, black terminal tail band. In both the literature and the hobby it is frequently confused with *Serrasalmus eigenmanni* and *S. serrulatus*, but both those species lack the tail band. In nature they are quite omnivorous, consuming fish plus seeds and fruit. The true *P. calmoni* is only occasionally imported, and almost always under an incorrect name. Conversely, many other species in the *S. eigenmanni/serrulatus* group (see above) are being regularly sold under the name of *P. calmoni*, so check for the presence of a black marginal tail band. Hobbyists should be on the lookout for a peculiar piranha of undetermined species that is occasionally being exported from Peru. Its appearance is in many ways intermediate

The disclike shape combined with the black tail band are distinct features of **Pristobrycon calmoni.**

between *S. serrulatus* and *P. calmoni*. A unique marking is a narrow, subterminal black band on the tail and anal fin. This fish might well turn out to be an undescribed species.

Pristobrycon aureus

Common name: None

Size: Not clearly understood, but most probably close to 8 inches (20 cm)

Distribution: The Guianas, and lower Amazon upstream as far as Manaus, Brazil. This is based on museum and university voucher specimens, some of which might not have been correctly attributed to this species.

Comments: *Pristobrycon aureus* is a particularly interesting species. It was originally rather poorly described in 1829 by Spix and Agassiz

with its range listed as the lower Amazon and Guiana rivers. The type specimens appear to have become lost, but several specimens purported to be this species have since been collected in Guiana and Brazil. Even though it has the generic characteristics of ectopterygoid teeth and a preanal spine, it has still been bounced back and forth between the genera *Pristobrycon* and *Serrasalmus*. Some authorities have suggested that it is a junior synonym of *S. eigenmanni*. Others, citing such differences as its yellow color ("aureus" means "yellow") and lack of a pronounced humeral spot, still consider it a valid species. One of the biggest surprises while writing this manuscript was receiving an e-mail with a photograph of a fish closely matching the original description and

This might actually be a photo of the real **Pristobrycon aureus,** *a fish that was very poorly described over 175 years ago.*

drawing of *P. aureus*. It was taken by Jared LeClercq, who had bought it from a pet store that claimed it was imported from Guiana. His photograph, reproduced here, is the only color photograph I have seen of a living fish that resembles *P. aureus*. There is no way of accurately determining the identity of this fish without having it in hand and carefully comparing the details of its anatomy with other related species and the original description. However, this specimen is tantalizing evidence that perhaps *Pristobrycon aureus* is a valid but rarely seen fish.

Pristobrycon maculipinnis

Common name: Marbled piranha; locally called piranha colorado, which translates into "red piranha"

Size: A large *Pristobrycon* attains a length of close to 12 inches (30 cm)

Distribution: Brazo Casiquiare, Rio Pamoni, and a tributary of the Atabapo River, Guiana Highlands, southern Venezuela

Comments: This most beautiful of the pristobrycons, and one of the most brilliantly colored of all piranhas, appears to have a very restricted range. As far as is known, it is a blackwater species. The rather deep and heavily mottled body is dark olive above, shading into rich orange-gold sides. The belly is an even richer red-orange. All fins except the pectorals are orange, becoming heavily speckled in adults. During the breeding season all colors intensify and the body displays blue and purple iridescence. Young are also quite orange, with prominent body spotting and mostly unmarked orange fins. It has been suggested that this species might be sexually dimorphic, with the outer edge of the female's anal fin being concave, whereas that of the male is gently

Pristobrycon maculipinnis is one of the most beautiful piranhas, as well as the largest known pristobrycon. This is a young specimen.

bilobed. Until many more specimens can be examined this remains unproven.

The diet of this fish is typical of the genus and comprises fish flesh and fins and a large amount of finely masticated seeds. It has been suggested that because this fish lacks a preanal

Adult P. maculipinnis *in spawning colors. Rio Pasimoni, Venezuela.*

spine and ectopterygoid teeth, it does not belong in the genus *Pristobrycon*.

This gorgeous fish is being imported in very small numbers. Because of its great beauty and the remoteness of its habitat its price is always extremely high. There are reports of it doing well when kept a short time with others of its own species, but considering its beauty, rarity, and high price, I do not think I would risk it.

Pristobrycon striolatus

Common names: Speckled piranha, black-tailed piranha

Size: 8 or 9 inches (20–23 cm)

Distribution: Orinoco and the lower and middle Amazon basins

Comments: Easily distinguished from all the other piranhas of discoid shape by the numerous small black speckles, rather than spots, that

Pristobrycon striolatus *is the only known piranha with such small, specklike spotting. Palm swamp near Rio Uracoa, Venezuela.*

decorate the upper half of its body. The basal area of the tail is marked with a conspicuous black V. In some parts of its range there is considerable orange-red pigment on the operculum and flanks. Young are more elongated and plain silvery in color with a bit of pink on the anal fin. Stomach content analysis has shown that smaller specimens feed primarily on fish fins, and adults shift to a diet primarily of masticated seeds and fish scales. The speckled piranha is imported only sporadically, and there is not much information about its aquarium care. Because of its fins and scale-eating tendencies I would recommend keeping it isolated from other fish, including others of its own kind.

As mentioned earlier, this species has lately generated quite a bit of discussion among taxonomists. It is described as a pristobrycon, but lacks the ectopterygoid teeth and preanal spine mentioned in this genus's original description. More controversial are the two recent studies that suggested that it be removed from *Pristobrycon* and placed in a new genus of its own. The jury is still out on this, but don't be surprised by name changes in the near future. This fish is not supposed to be found in the upper Amazon region of Peru, but in the last few years a fish closely resembling this species has occasionally been caught in the Rio Nanay outside of Iquitos, Peru.

Genus *Pygopristis*

This monotypic genus is notable for its unusual, multicusped tooth anatomy. Their

Male (above) five-cusped piranhas can be differentiated from females (below) by the convex outer edge of the anal fin.

unique tooth structure may be an adaptation for their diet of seeds. Adults are sexually dimorphic, an uncommon characteristic in piranhas but seen frequently in other genera of serrasalmins. Males can be identified by a fuller dorsal fin and lobed anal fin. This unusual fish is thought to be most closely related to *Pristobrycon striolatus* and *Catoprion mento*.

Pygopristis denticulata

Common name: Five-cusped piranha
Size: 10 inches (25 cm)
Distribution: Orinoco and Amazon basins, including the Peruvian Amazon, and the north and east Guiana Highland rivers

Comments: The five-cusped piranha is blunt-faced and high backed, with a convex dorsal and ventral profile. In color it is usually some shade of greenish-yellow, frequently overlaid with darker mottling arranged in vertical stripes. A diffuse dark spot is usually present on the posterior portion of the gill plate, and the basal half of the tail is black. The unpaired fins are tinted orange and the anal fin is often finely edged with light blue. In some parts of its range there may be considerable orange on the operculum and lower sides. Very darkly colored specimens are sometimes caught. *Pygopristis* prefers clear- or blackwater habitats, and is generally absent from whitewater rivers.

This fish is much less predatory than any other piranha. Analysis of stomach contents showed that young fish between $1\frac{1}{2}$ and $3\frac{1}{4}$ inches (4 and 8 cm) fed almost entirely on seeds that were thoroughly masticated before being swallowed. With maturity seeds and scales were consumed in equal amounts with smaller amounts of aquatic insects.

It has only recently been discovered that this fish's range includes Peru, and I have seen specimens caught in the Rio Nanay and a blackwater tributary of the Rio Napo. It is starting to be imported with greater frequency, most often under an incorrect name. Checking the shape of its teeth is a foolproof method of correctly identifying this fish. Look for it in mixed piranha shipments coming out of Iquitos, Peru, during the rainy season (November–March).

Five-cusped piranhas have been successfully kept in aquariums with its serrasalmin relatives of the genera *Metynnis* and *Mylossoma*.

Most five-cusped piranhas will readily accept chopped fish and shrimp, but it is recommended that to keep them in optimum health a large amount of vegetable matter be included in their diet. Frank Magallanes has had great success feeding wild-bird seed to his *Pygopristis*. They even searched out seeds that sank to the bottom. I can find no records of it being bred in an aquarium. It would be interesting to learn whether it pairs and protects its eggs as with all other piranhas for which we have reproductive data, or simply scatters its eggs among vegetation, as is the case with the related silver dollars.

Genus *Catoprion*

This is another monotypic genus, with *Catoprion mento*, the wimpel piranha, being its sole member.

Catoprion mento

Common name: Wimpel piranha (usually misspelled wimple)

Size: Less than 6 inches (15 cm); smaller than most piranhas

Distribution: Orinoco, lower and middle Amazon basin, south to Bolivia. Absent from the Peruvian Amazon

Comments: Until recently this was not considered a true piranha, but this opinion might have to be changed if recent findings prove correct. The commonly seen spelling "wimple" is incorrect. *Wimpel* is a German word that means a "banner" or "pennant," and alludes to the filamentous extensions of the dorsal and anal fins of adult specimens. This unusual fish is basically olive-green in color. Some specimens display an orange blotch on the operculum, and most adults have the anterior rays of the dorsal and anal fin greatly extended. At all ages its lower jaw is markedly prognathic. The wimpel piranha's diet is made up almost exclusively of

A particularly beautiful wimpel piranha with undamaged fin extensions. San Martin River, Bolivia.

fish scales, and its peculiar, everted, and tubercular teeth are adapted for efficiently removing scales from its prey.

Aquarium experiences have shown that young wimpel piranhas under 2 inches (5 cm) in length may get along quite well together, but adults show extreme conspecific aggression and must be kept by themselves. Their diet of scales precludes any attempts to keep them with other fish—unless they are intended as food. Aquarium specimens do not demand a diet of scales, and will quickly learn to accept small pieces of fish and shrimp, frozen bloodworms, and small krill (*Euphasia pacifica*). Adults will also accept whole small dead or living fish the size of guppies or mosquitofish (*Gambusia affinis*). It has not been observed breeding in nature, and I can find no records of it spawning in an aquarium.

INFORMATION

Web Sites

Oregon Piranha Exotic Fish Exhibit (OPEFE)
http://www.opefe.com/
   The best Internet source for up-to-date information about piranhas

Piranha–Fury
http://www.piranha-fury.com/
   An online forum about all aspects of piranhas and piranha care

Books

Géry, J. 1977. *Characoids of the World*. Neptune City, NJ: TFH Publications.

Goulding, M. 1980. *The Fishes and the Forest: Explorations in Amazonian Natural History*. Los Angeles: University of California Press.

Machado-Allison, A. 1987. *Los Peces de los Llanos de Venezuela: Un esayo sobre su historia natural*. Caracas, Venezuela: Universida Central de Venezuela.

Myers, G., (ed.) 1972. *The Piranha Book: An Account of the Ill-famed Piranha Fishes of the Rivers of Tropical South America.* Neptune City, NJ: TFH Publications.

Noga, J. E. 2000. *Fish Disease: Diagnosis and Treatment*. Ames, IA: Blackwell Publishing Professional.

Schulte, W. 1988. *Piranhas in the Aquarium*: Neptune City, NJ: TFH Publications.

References

Freeman, B., L. G. Nico, M. Osentoski, H. L. Jelks, and T. M. Collins. 2007. Molecular systematics of Serrasalminae: Deciphering the identities of piranha species and unraveling their evolutionary histories. *Zootaxa* 1484: 1–38.

Hubert, N., F. Duponchelle, J. Nuñez, C. Garcia-Davilla, D. Paugy, and J. Francois Renno. Phylogeny of the Piranha genera *Serrasalmus* and *Pygocentrus*: Implications for the diversification of the Neotropical ichthyofauna. Molecular Ecology (2007): 1–22.

Machado-Allison, A. 1985. Estudios sobre la sistemática de las subfamilia Serrasalminae. Part III: Sobre el estaus génerico y relationses filogeneticaus de los géneros Pygopristis, Pygocentrus, Pristobrycon y Serrasalmus (Teleostei-Characidae). *Acta Biologica Venezuelica* 12(1): 19–42.

Machado-Allison, A. and C. Garcia. 1986. Food Habits and Morphological Changes during Antogeny in Three Serrasalmin Fish Species of the Venezuelan Floodplains. *Copeia* 1986 (1): 193–196.

Sazima, I. and S. de Andrade Guimaraes. 1987. Scavenging on Human Corpses as a Source for Stories about Maneating Piranhas. *Environmental Biology of Fishes* 20(1): 75–77.

Winemiller, K. O. 1990. Caudal Eyespots as Deterrents against Fin Predation in the Neotropical Cichlid *Astronotus ocellatus*. *Copeia* 1990 (3): 665–673.

Tables of Equivalents and Conversions

Equivalents

one centimeter (cm) equals 100 millimeters (mm)
one foot (ft) equals 12 inches (in)
one gallon (gal) equals 32 ounces (oz)
one kilogram (kg) equals 1,000 grams (gm)
one milliliter (ml) equals (approximately) 25 drops
one tablespoon equals 3 teaspoons

Conversions

Temperature: Multiply Celsius (°C) by 1.8, then subtract 32 to obtain Fahrenheit (°F).
Subtract 32 from Fahrenheit, then multiply by 0.55 to obtain Celsius.

Measurement	multiplied by	equals
centimeters	0.4	inches
inches	2.54	centimeters
feet	30.0	centimeters
liters	1.06	quarts
quarts	0.95	liters
gallons	3.8	liters
pounds	0.45	kilograms

Important Note

Anyone keeping piranhas as pets must use extreme caution at all times when handling them or servicing their aquarium. The razor-sharp teeth and powerful jaws of large piranhas are able to inflict severe flesh wounds, and are even capable of cleanly amputating a finger. For this reason, hobbyists with small children are strongly advised not to keep piranhas as pets. A doctor should immediately be seen for the treatment of any severe piranha bite.

When electrical appliances are used in the presence of water, there is always the potential for life-threatening accidents.

- Purchase only electrical equipment that has been tested and approved by Underwriters Laboratory (UL).
- Carefully read all operating instructions.
- Always use a ground fault interrupter device that will automatically turn off appliances plugged into them if they develop a short circuit or malfunction.
- Turn off all electrical devices before servicing your aquarium.
- If you should ever experience an electrical shock when you touch your aquarium or any of its equipment, immediately unplug all electrical devices until the source of the problem can be identified.
- Promptly discard, or have repaired by a reputable electrician, any piece of faulty electrical equipment.

About the Author

David M. Schleser was trained as a dentist, and practiced dentistry for 19 years. In 1982 he changed careers to aquatic biology, and later served for more than five years as the curator/aquatic biologist for the Dallas Aquarium, Dallas, Texas. He retired from this position to work full time for Nature's Images, Inc., a natural history photography, graphic design, and writing company that he helped establish. Since 1988, David has traveled regularly to the rain forests of Costa Rica and the Amazon regions of Peru and Brazil for purposes of research and photography. He frequently serves as the tour leader for Amazon River photographic and tropical fish study expeditions. David Schleser's photographs and writings have appeared in many scientific and popular publications. He also presents many lectures on aquatic subjects to aquarium societies throughout the United States and Canada. His major ichthyologic interests are South American characins, the Centrarchids of North America, and desert fishes.

Acknowledgments

First and foremost I would like to thank Frank Magallanes for sharing his immense knowledge of piranhas, referring me to some top piranha field biologists and hobbyists worldwide, and providing me with many excellent photographs. Ivan Mikolji kindly sent me excellent photographs of several rare and local Venezuelan piranhas plus their habitats. Dr. Leo Nico permitted me access to his (unpublished) doctoral dissertation on piranha ecology, provided photographs of some lesser-known piranha species; Dr. Kirk O. Winemiller sent me copies of many papers he and others authored concerning piranha biology and natural history, and graciously supplied me with some excellent photographs used in this book; Dr. William Fink supplied reprints of his papers about piranha taxonomy and helped in the identification of specimens collected during my South American travels. I would also like to thank Dr. Antonio Machado-Allison for sharing with me some of his opinions concerning piranha taxonomy and species identification, as well as providing me with several important photographs. Other people who graciously permitted me to use some of their excellent photographs are Janelle Barron, Alex Casas, Jeff Concannon, Anthony Christodoulov, Claudia Dickerson, George Fear of Shark Aquarium, Jared LeClercq, Edouard Paiva, Ashley Peters, Jerry Plakyda, Brandon Rogers of Rogers Aquatic, Aaron Shames, Alex Uttley, Mark Van Broek, Jay Vallee, and Raul Yalan of Neotropical Fauna. Dr. Stanley Weitzman was, as always, a tremendous help in discussing questions involving characoid taxonomy. A special thanks to Roger Klocek for information concerning captive reproduction of various piranha species at the Shedd Aquarium. David T. and Mary Roberts proofread the first draft of the manuscript and provided many important suggestions. Last, but not least, I cannot thank enough the many people I met in my visits to the Amazon region who, though too numerous to individually name, were indispensable in the obtaining of needed specimens and providing me with firsthand knowledge about piranhas.

Cover Photos

Front, inside front, and inside back covers by Shutterstock. Back cover: Ivan Mikolji.

Photo Credits

Nature's Images, Inc.: 2–3, 4, 6 (left), 7, 8, 12 (bottom), 15, 16 (bottom), 17 (left & right), 18, 19, 20, 21 (left), 22 (right), 24, 26 (top, bottom left, bottom right), 27, 28, 29, 30, 33 (top & bottom), 35, 37, 38, 46, 47, 49, 50, 54, 55, 56, 57, 59, 61, 62, 63 (top & bottom), 64, 65, 66 (top left & right), 67, 69 (bottom), 70, 71, 75, 77 (top), 80, 83 (left), 84 (top); Ivan Mikolji: 13 (top left and right), 21 (right), 25 (top), 72, 73, 82, 88; George Fear/Shark Aquarium: 6 (right), 10, 22 (left), 68, 84 (bottom), 85; Jeff Cardwell: 74 (top & bottom), 91; Frank Magallanes: 13 (bottom right), 16 (top), 66 (bottom), 69 (top); Dr. Kirk Winemiller: 11, 76, 87 (bottom); Dr. Antonio Machado-Allison: 14, 77 (bottom); Adrien Leroy: 43, 79 (top & bottom); Aaron Shames: 39, 51; Jeff Concannon: 44, 78; Brandon Rogers: 5; Edouard Paiva: 9; Claudia Dickerson: 12 (top); Anthony Christodoulou: 25 (bottom); Alex Casas: 81; Raul Yalan: 83 (right), 89 (bottom); Jared LeClercq: 86; Ashley Peters: 87 (top); James McChancy: 89 (top); Jerry Plakyda: 58; Mark van den Broek: 42.

All inquiries should be addressed to:
Barron's Educational Series, Inc.
250 Wireless Boulevard
Hauppauge, NY 11788
www.barronseduc.com

ISBN-13: 978-0-7641-3958-1
ISBN-10: 0-7641-3958-4

Library of Congress Catalog Card No. 2008004799

Library of Congress Cataloging-in-Publication Data
Schleser, David M.
    Piranhas / by David M. Schleser. — 2nd ed.
        p. cm. — (A complete pet owner's manual)
    Includes bibliographical references and index.
    ISBN-13: 978-0-7641-3958-1 (alk. paper)
    ISBN-10: 0-7641-3958-4 (alk. paper)
    1. Piranhas. I. Title.

SF458.P57S36 2008
636.3'748—dc22   2008004799

Printed in China
9 8 7 6 5 4 3 2 1